ONTHEBUS

issue 24

ONTHEBUS

issue 24

Bambaz Press / Bombshelter Press
Los Angeles 2020

ONTHEBUS + FRE&D

not the last issue 24   issue 4 / art insert

EDITOR-IN-CHIEF
BAMBI HERE

CREATIVE DIRECTOR
BAZ HERE

EDITOR EMERITUS
JACK GRAPES

EDITOR-AT-LARGE
LINDA NEAL

ISBN: 9798615478079

Cover photograph by Baz Here

Bambaz Press / Bombshelter Press
www.bambazpress.com
bambi@bambazpress.com

548 S. Spring Street 1201
Los Angeles, California 90013 USA
Printed in the United States of America

Live to the point of tears.

–Albert Camus

from *Rendesvouz*, Portrait of Rembrandt with a Gorget Reimagined

CONTENTS

IN MEMORIAM

FROM THE EDITORS

TEAM BUS

TEACHER TEACHER

POETRY & PROSE

FRE&D

IN MEMORIAM

GLADYS LOVE SMITH
–Gladys Love Smith was the mother of Elvis Presley

On a double bed in a corner
of a white shingled shotgun house
in Tupelo, Mississippi
she pushes down hard,

so hard everyone is surprised
when the second boy appears.
She's gone to church
every Sunday, she has the gift,

God coming through, the Holy Laugh,
she can speak in tongues.
Both boys heard her,
but only one survived birth,

the one who heard the sound from afar,
the rock & roll of a rattlesnake guitar.

WHAT IS IT LIKE TO BE BEETHOVEN?
I'm trying to hear
the sonic landscape
of his mind,
the sounds of violins,
viola & cello—
a string quartet of
consciousness.
But I can't hear
those sounds
anymore
than I can
imagine
what it's like
to hang
upside down
all day
then dart
about at dusk
chasing insects
I can't see,
only hear.

FROM THE EDITORS

Look at the pretty people in the painterly portraits in this issue[1]—their beautiful wardrobes, evoking the opulence, the wealth, and the privilege—like France in the 18th century. The Baroque period was coming to an end, the church was no longer the only driving force for the arts—and similar to our current sociopolitical landscape, the divide between the rich and the poor was extraordinary. The Rococo artists were interested in grandiose ideals and lust for the aristocratic lifestyle—the entitlement of the rich.

And while all the frivolity and sumptuous going-on's were occurring in the palace, who was just down the street in the alleys, huddled and hungry? The disenfranchised. The saying, "Let them eat cake" comes to mind. The attribution is ambiguous—it is often said that Marie Antoinette uttered it. That may not be true. However, now our understanding of that phrase is a reflection of the disdain of the upper classes—oblivious and selfish—dismissive of the plight of the peasants right below the palace.

Have times changed? No. Our homeless population has become pandemic. The continuous building of high rises offers sanctuary for those who can afford the lifestyle. Yet, where is housing for the homeless? As the privileged continue to renovate or reimagine spaces into their hipster coffee shops, trendy art galleries, and luxury condominiums, this gentrification becomes an assault on the thousands of homeless who call places like Skid Row home.

According to Selena Larson at *CNN Business*, "Walking through any neighborhood in San Francisco is a visual reminder of the city's inequality. Almost 7,000 adults are homeless, and tent encampments are set up amongst the world's biggest tech companies and million-dollar apartments."[2] The city wanted to clear out all the homeless before the Super Bowl. The dilemma continues.

"Finding the political will to build shelters across California is one thing. Finding a way to force homeless people to use those shelters ... will be quite another. Still, it's a discussion worth having, as people continue to waste away on our streets,"[3] says editor Erika Smith, *LA Times*.

And now, what about the 2028 Los Angeles Olympics? What kind of impact will these games have on our city? Does the post-olympic disaster of Rio and Brazil serve as a warning? The dangers of a city's broken aftermath are a real concern.

"Eight years from now, when Los Angeles shows itself off again on the world stage, authorities will have two options, says Jody Armour, a law professor at USC who studies crime and culture. 'They could opt for a more cosmetic approach,' he says. 'Or they could do something concrete and substantive that addresses the lack of affordable housing and the lack of adequate jobs and mental health services.'"[4]

"It's an honor to host the Olympics, but we have to rise to a recognition that everyone in our city is a neighbor," Jones says. "We need to provide real solutions to poverty and homelessness and not just make people disappear because it's convenient."[3] –Jerry Jones, director of public policy at Inner City Law Center.

By presenting these painterly photographic portraits by Baz Here reminiscent of the grandeur of the Rococo, the drawings of homeless by Richard Gayler, and the incredible life-changing stories and poetry from Urban Possiblities, we hope to create a conversation. The need for shelter and kindness is calling all of us to pay attention. Aren't those people in tents, sitting on the corners, asking for money our neighbors, too? Can we delight ourselves in luxuries and leisure (like olympic games) all while cultivating an attitude of social responsibility? No one should be left behind. All of us, the one percent, the shrinking middle, the poor, and the homeless have a story worth hearing.

I've learned that people will forget what you said,
people will forget what you did,
but people will never forget how you made them feel.

–Maya Angelou

---

1   Rococo inspired painterly photographic portraits found on the cover and pages 15,18,27,37, and 75.
2   Larson, Selena. "San Francisco's Tech Elite Fund Measure To Ban Homeless Camps". Cnnmoney, 2020, https://money.cnn.com/2016/10/14/technology/tents-homeless-ban-san-francisco/index.html.
3   Smith, Erika. "In 2019, Homelessness Truly Felt Like A Crisis In Every Corner Of L.A.". Los Angeles Times, 2020, https://www.latimes.com/california/story/2019-12-10/homeless-housing-crisis-los-angeles.
4   Chandler, Jenna. "How Will LA Treat The Homeless When It Hosts The Olympics In 2028?". Curbed LA, 2020, https://la.curbed.com/2018/7/12/17454676/los-angeles-olympics-homeless-police-militarization-security.

Photo: Baz Here

FEATURED BOOK: *PADDLE TO PADDLE*

LOIS CHAPIN (NIGHTINGALE ROSE PUBLICATIONS, 2019)

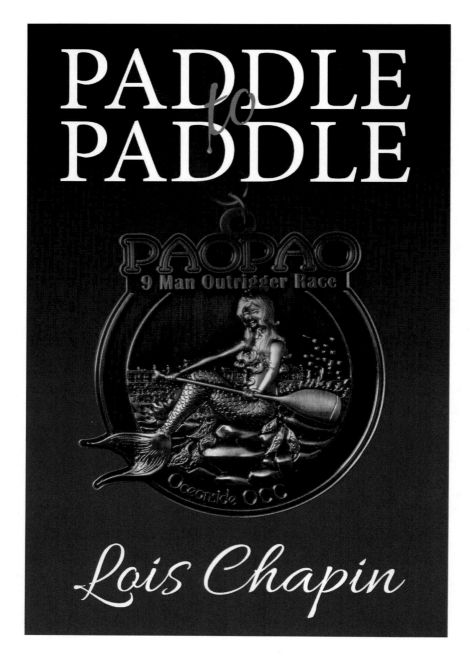

"*Paddle to Paddle* is eclectic and electric, filled with taboos and secrets, perfect for reflective consumption that acts as a form of therapy, as well as a work of poetic artistry."

Self-Publishing Review

"It's resonating personal message and pragmatic feminism are powerfully compelling."

Manhattan Book Review

"I enjoyed this poetry book—more than I've enjoyed a poetry book in a long time. I am looking forward to more work from Chapin."

Seattle Book Review

MARGARET TYNES FAIRLEY (BAMBAZ PRESS, 2019)

You, dear reader, have the good fortune to experience a master poet: she who tucks metaphors into the emotional chaos of nature, uncovers our tender connection with an illusory world, rendering her words into seasons of sea, flowers, birds, and trees. I believe Margaret Tynes Fairley is one of the most accomplished poets of the 20th Century – as yet an "undiscovered" writer to a wider audience – but she should hold the place of a historic poet in the 1920s and 1930s, shaping metaphors and images into an enduring substance.

Photo: Baz Here

TEAM BUS

WHY WRITE POETRY?
You've probably asked yourself
that same question when you get up in the morning,
even before you think about
what you'll have for breakfast,
Well, to be more accurate, we should ask,
"Why write a poem?"
Poetry takes in a lot of things.
Writing poetry is a commitment,
a life,
but a poem, a single poem,
why even bother?
Anything can be poetry.
You don't have to commit to a thing
to recognize poetry.
Poetry is all around us, everywhere we look.
The way a leaf falls to the ground.
You watch it and exclaim:
"That's poetry."
We've all stopped in our tracks
to watch a beautiful sunset.
A road sign, for instance, can be poetry.
I was driving alone one time
on one of those two-lane,
asphalt, back country highways,
middle of the night
in the great state of Georgia
on my way to visit my buddy
who was stationed in the Army
out in the field somewhere around Macon,
and I fell asleep at the wheel.
See, here I am in the middle of *this* poem
talking about a road sign
that was all lit up like Times Square
and before I can get past thirty-two lines
it strikes me that even the expression
asleep at the wheel
jumps out at me as poetry.
See, the point is, if you really think about it,
poetry can stop you in your tracks
even while you're washing the dishes,
or asleep at the wheel.
Poetry can stop you in your tracks
even when you're in the middle
of writing a poem.
He was asleep at the wheel.
She was unconscious at the tiller.
They were snoozing at the throttle.
He caught a few Z's at the controls.
Life may not side-track you

Poetry is all around us,
everywhere we look.
The way a leaf falls to the ground.
You watch it and exclaim:
"That's poetry."

if you've got a focused will,
but poetry will do that to you every time.
That seems to be the heroic act
you perform as a poet,
not to get sidetracked by the poem.
He got sidetracked by the poem.
She got hoodwinked by the sonnet.
They got spoonfed by the haiku.
We got hi-jacked by the sestina.
See what I mean?
Don't get sidetracked by the poem.

Anyway, where was I?
Oh, yeah, asleep at the wheel,
on an old, two-lane highway
around midnight
somewhere in the middle of Georgia
between Augusta and Alexander City,
when I woke with a start.
I was going about 75 miles per hour
heading straight for a huge road sign,
all lit up
in the middle of that pitch black darkness
on a spit of land
between the spot where the highway forked,
left for Milledgeville,
right for Waynesboro.
For a moment, I thought I was parked
in a drive-in movie,
a cinemascope film right beyond my windshield.
In the next moment, hardly the flicker of a second
I realized I was heading straight for that billboard
– or was it heading straight for me? –
the silent voice of God proclaiming:
"PREPARE TO MEET ETERNITY!"
All my sins –
failed promises,
lackluster liasons,
pathetic platitudes,
devious procrastinations,
disemboweled friendships,
carnivorous betrayals –
all of them flashed before my eyes
as my car sped straight
for the glowing movie screen,
door luring me into this semblance of eternity.
Where the hell was I?
I did a quick calculation:
I was on my way to Macon,
smack dab in the middle of the state,
population 153,000,
home of the Allman Brothers Band Museum
and those Native American earthen mounds

That seems to be the heroic act
you perform as a poet,
not to get sidetracked
by the poem.

dating back to 1,000 AD
in the Ocmulgee National Monument.
There's exhibits on African-American art,
history and culture

in the Harriet Tubman Museum
on Cherry Street,
the largest museum of its kind
just across from the Georgia Sports Hall of Fame,
right next door to the Tic Toc Room,
an upscale steakhouse
where I once had, what they called,
a "creative martini."
Does it snow in Macon? Zero inches per year.
Does it rain in Macon? Thirty-eight inches per year.
Cost of living? Median home is $74,000.
Macon also has the highest crime rate
in America compared to all communities
of all sizes – 56 per 1,000 residents;
your chance of becoming a victim
of either violent or property crime
is one in 18.
So unless I planned
to plow through that billboard
toward Eternity,
I either had to turn left toward Milledgeville
or right toward Waynesboro.
Which one led to Macon?
My brain was working overtime
in those fractions of a second,
making so many calculations upon calculations,
that my high-school calculus teacher
would have been proud to see
so much smoke coming out of my ears.
"What if I just keep going straight,"
I thought, "right into that billboard,
all lit up like it was a portal
in some sci-fi fantasy film."
Eternity.
It didn't say death, just "eternity."
And the philosopher-poet in me
spared myself one more split fraction of a second
to think about what it said –
not that by plowing through that sign
I'd head into eternity –
that's not quite what the sign said.
What the fucking sign said,
all lit up in the middle of nowhere,
was that I had to *PREPARE*
to meet eternity.
Right there in that car,
I had to *prepare* to meet eternity,
asleep at the wheel,

Right there in that car,
I had to prepare
to meet eternity,
asleep at the wheel,

going 75 miles an hour
on a back road two-lane highway
around midnight in Georgia
on my way to Macon to visit my buddy
who was in the army stationed
out in the field doing maneuvers in the mud,
where we were going to put on a comedy show
for the troops, which we did,
on a flatbed truck in the eye of a hurricane,
which is another story altogether.
But there I was, being told to "prepare"
to meet Eternity. *Prepare.*
Well, it took another split second
for me to opt for Milledgeville,
a sudden quarter-turn of the wheel
and I was on my way to Milledgeville,
population 250.
But the point I was going to make –
before I got sidetracked at the wheel –
was that poetry could be anything,
anywhere, a torn scrap of a letter,
a tv commercial, a paragraph in a novel,
a marriage proposal on a cruise ship,
lego instructions in a box,
etcetera, etcetera, etcetera.
Poetry is everywhere.
To invoke the clichéd analogy,
you could be anywhere in your life
and up pops poetry.
So my point is,
the question is not: "Why write poetry?"
The question is "Why write a poem?"
That's the more important question.
Why a poem, and not a story
or a novel or a play or a song.
Why a poem?
Is there anything in this world
more inconsequential
than a poem?
Compared to the Taj Mahal
or *Gone with the Wind*
or Shostakovitch's *5th Symphony*
in D minor, Op. 47, first performed
in Leningrad in 1937,
receiving an ovation that lasted over half an hour
with people running like crazy
out into the snow-covered streets still cheering,
compared to that,
a poem is just a piece of confetti.
And yet?
Some of us think about that
when we wake up in the morning,
even before we think about

To invoke the clichéd analogy,
you could be anywhere
in your life and up pops poetry.

what we're going to have for breakfast.
Why write a poem?
Why go to Milledgeville, Georgia,
population 250,
when Eternity is all lit up,
calling you, imploring you,
begging you,
desperate for your puny soul,
as it travels 75 miles per hour
in the middle of the night
on a dark, back-country,
two-lane highway
on your way to Macon,
in the great state of Georgia?

BAMBI HERE

ENTERING EARTH

I saw a shooting star
on my computer screen reflection
except I was looking sideways—to my left
at the sky place between the curtains.
I mean—it's like when we are looking away
but know we saw it anyway—that kind of thing.
Blink and it goes—gone.
That's why I prefer aluminum foil
to Saran Wrap—
I can't see that the cheese
has already molded.
These bits of falling light
were just dust and rock,
not even stars—
they were mummies really—
meteoroids tumbling
into the equations of atmosphere
disappearing to earth.
That evanescent shimmering
illuminated the magnanimity
of innocent children.
They don't know that we only see the light
when the shooting star dies.
Waiting for rocks to boink me on my head
is silly, just silly—even my kids didn't worry
about that. They were more worried
about that witch
who lived under their beds.
I decided in that moment,
that very fleeting moment,
that only moment,
we will all move to Scotland
and gather fallen rocks.

Waiting for rocks to boink me
on my head is silly,
just silly—even my kids
didn't worry about that.

THE WALKER
If you were to remove my shoe now,
if you were to remove my sock,
if you were to remove my foot from the floor,
the heel in your left hand, the ball in your right,
you would touch moist skin only minor calluses
trimmed toenails and the scent of frankincense and myrhh.

You might imagine the soles of my shoes walking the streets of DTLA,
in sync with the black dog—left right pause for a poo and a sniff—
down Broadway past the donut shop and the Spring Arcade.
You might see my smile towering above my Red Nikes
offering you a nice day and a kiss on the cheek.
You may catch us (me and the dog) at Pershing Square, airpods in,
chatting with Mom about her TV shows.
You might find us at Walgreens, buying coconut water and M&M's.
You might see us (and to clarify, just me and the dog)
happy.

If you were to remove my shoes,
take off my socks,
place my foot in your hands,
it would be impossible for you to see
when we weren't walking,

it would be impossible for you to know
the moments in between
the trips with the dog
between the loft where I work
and the loft where I sleep.
It would be impossible for you to feel
the weight on my back...

y'know—most would pack their bag
when they leave for the day
for the trips in between.

But I arrive, at my home.
I arrive at my studio.
I arrive and put my backpack on.

If you were to remove my sock,
you would see my pretty feet,
since I only stand in one place
when I hold the weight
in my backpack on my back—
when I arrive and let them know,
I am here.

You might see my smile
towering above my Red Nikes
offering you a nice day
and a kiss on the cheek.

MARRIAGE TRACT
–after Catherine Pierce

In the beginning, marriage was a delicious ceremony,
midsummer amid pines, needles softening underfoot,
followed by new percale sheets,
smoothed onto a hand-me-down double bed
where laughter and sex-wet nights rained down.
We'd heard that the migration of days
would dull the lust, but not that the dryness
would come so early. When long nights of love-making
became long days of clocks and books and a typewriter
on the breakfast table. When the breakfast table
became the lunch table, the dinner table,
the baby changing table by the bassinette.
When I won at cribbage, and he threw
his coffee mug against the wall.
One New Year's Eve I wrestled with an ear ache
and my guilt for keeping us at home.
At least you're learning how to cook, he said.
An absurd comfort. The baby cried.
The baby grew into a boy. Another came.
And the house with the lemon tree
and a view of the Pacific. But we never saw
the world through the same kaleidoscope,
even as we both saw the dog
eat the lemons that ruined his teeth,
and we both loved sitting at the edge
of the ocean in matching beach chairs.
We said we would hold on to the dirt
of marriage, hold on to it for life,
until we were hanging on for dear life. No one said,
Sorry, I'm so sorry, I'm so very sorry. The marriage bled
until it became a wound we could not close.

Tampa Review, "Marriage Tract" (10th Prize, *Writer's Digest contest,* 2018)

Photo: Baz Here

TEACHER TEACHER

THIRTEEN WAYS TO LOOK AT THE MOON
–after Wallace Stevens' "Thirteen Ways of Looking at a Blackbird"

The first way to look at the moon
is straight up
with a shot of whiskey on the side.

The second would be through
the site of a rifle,
a man on his knees.

The third, of course, is skipping
along the embryonic trail,
throwing starlight
to find your way back.

The fourth would be to plant a rose bush
on the sunny side of the hill,
the side that overlooks the corral
where you keep the horse
you rode in on.

You could look at the moon through a hole
in the middle of a slice
of buttered bread,

or through slits between the fingers
of the hand you've raised to cover
your eyes,
the moon's beauty too great to bear
in an oversized tee
and bare feet.

Of the seventh, well, it's the one
to come back to after you've been
away and returned.

Eighth is to point at her, arm outstretched.
Then take someone's hand and say,
"The incidence of candlelight
might make a pawn tremble
with delight."

The ninth way is to be the pawn.

Way number ten would be not
to look
at the moon, but to look
at the stillness of the dark lake instead.

> the moon's beauty
> too great to bear
> in an oversized tee

A circle drawn on a piece of paper
might be the moon. Look at it that way.

Or whisper her name
in every language you know.

The twelfth way to look at the moon
is to re-assemble the apple slices
in your piece of pie.

Thirteen is the moon watches you.

KEVIN JACOBSEN

THINKING AND WATCHING
I fell a lot as a kid. My knees
always bruised and scratched
in the summer. I liked riding
my bike fast down the hill
by the slaughterhouse. When
the truck was parked on the right
side of the slaughterhouse,
by the metal ramp, that went
up to the red metal door, I
knew an animal was going
to die. Sometimes, I'd watch
the animal see daylight for
the last time. Stumbling and soiling
the metal ramp on its way up
to the red door. I stood there
thinking, and watching, gripping
the cold-grooved handlebars
on my bike. I had one foot on
the ground, thinking and watching
the animal disappear,
and the red door to the slaughter
house slammed shut. Some cars
went by. No one I knew. I just
stood there, thinking and watching,
wondering what I would do when
I got big. Then I heard the metal
shoot, and I pictured the warm
animal's body on the cold concrete
floor. I'd seen it once before
when the red door was left open.
I got on my bike and pedaled fast
down the hill. I turned right by
the green mailboxes and the milk-ramp.
Then onto the dirt road to home,
sending up a cloud of dust. I wanted
to write something good.
Something that made me cry.

I wanted
to write something good.
Something that made me cry.

Something that made you cry.
Something you'd remember.
So, I wrote this instead.

DIRTY WORK

dead crow on the roots
of her mother's tree, its eye
a thriving anthill.

i wait on the curb
only weeks before the end.
call it an omen.

only the crow knows
how to bury the body
and set the soul free.

crow left noah's hand
and made the broken world whole
right under god's nose.

he keeps his secrets.
he knows the dirtiest work
is holiest too.

only the crow knows
how to bury the body

TRUE PRAYER
As soon as the man is one with God, he will not beg.
–Ralph Waldo Emerson

At the Basilica in Rome,
I fell to my knees
my palms face down,
my forehead between them,
and let my tears pool
on the green-veined marble floor.
My grey summer dress spread
around me like a cathedral bell.
I did not believe in any God,
but something inside, something
I recognized, believed in me.

True prayer is not blind faith.
It asks for nothing outside itself.
No separate God to save us,
no deity or supreme being

to soften the way, to heal,
to weigh itself under confession.

True prayer is a turning inward,
a knowing that God is the substance
of all consciousness,
that even air is part of God.

True prayer is an empty mind,
the space beyond conditioning or belief,
that pinprick of light inside us all,
patient and waiting only for itself.

True prayer is a responsibility,
where suffering and unrequited desires
melt like ice under flame
when one ceases soliciting from God.

True prayer is the sanctuary of awareness,
the knowing that I am both the prayer
and the answer to my prayer.

> let my tears pool
> on the green-veined marble floor.

CAROLYN ZIEL

MARRIAGE ON HER SKIN

Her husband woke her. Sarah had been dreaming about mornings, and how she used to open herself up, pink petal by pink petal, warm, wet, soft. In her dream, she was spinning color. Like that game she loved when she was a girl, the one with the paints and the spinning wheel. Her husband was standing in the doorway to their bedroom. He was dressed in jeans, a t-shirt, and a leather jacket. The light in the hallway backlit him so she couldn't see his face.

She sat up, pulling the sheet with her, tucking it under her arms. She was naked. They had made love earlier that evening, and she could still feel the warmth of their marriage on her skin. She glanced at the clock on her bedside table, 4 am. She looked back at her husband. She didn't know how long he'd been standing there. She thought maybe she was still dreaming because of the girl sitting on the floor between them. Her husband wasn't paying any attention to the girl. Sometimes Sarah felt like he didn't pay much attention to her either. If he could see the girl, that would mean Sarah wasn't dreaming. She wanted to ask him if he did, but knew that it would upset him, especially if the girl wasn't there.

She knew her husband was talking to her, but she didn't know what he was saying because her ears were buzzing and all the color from her dream was still swishing around in her head. And the girl was humming. Smiling and humming and playing with Sarah's favorite spin art game. The girl was wearing a pink dress with tiny white polka dots. Her hair was pulled back into a ponytail and was tied with a pink and white ribbon. Sarah worried that she might get paint on her dress.

Her husband's words were coming at her now, faster and faster. Viscous globs of color blasting by her, splashing the walls and the ceilings. Blue, red, green, black, yellow, splotches on the carpet and the bedsheets and the pillows, blobs of color on her naked arms, cheeks and in her hair. She wanted his words to stop, wanted the buzzing to stop, wanted her heart to stop pounding and thumping in her ears. She wanted quiet. Her husband didn't seem to notice the mess he was making with his words or that a few of them almost hit the girl on the floor.

Sarah pulled her attention away from the mess and the girl and looked at her husband standing in the doorway. That's when she noticed that he was holding his overnight bag. That his wallet, keys, money clip, and the small pocketknife he left on his dresser each night were gone. His wedding ring was still there. Sarah liked the simplicity of their wedding rings. Two gold bands that symbolized the circle of their love, a love that would go on, with no beginning and no end. Till death do us part.

"It's over," her husband said. "I'm leaving."

She wanted to run to him, throw herself in his arms, wrap herself around him, hold him tight, never let go, but she wasn't dressed and didn't want the little girl to see her nakedness. She hugged her arms around her legs and squeezed tight. She closed her eyes and listened to her husband walk down the hallway, listened to his footsteps echo through the house, listened to the click of the front door open and then close. Then he drove away. And it was quiet. Sarah opened her eyes. She was glad to see that the girl was still there, humming and smiling and spinning her colors. Glad that she wasn't alone.

NATALIE SKORYKOVA

RED LION MASK

They promised to give me my Red Lion.

I thought it was a red dragon, but the chef explained to me that it was a Japanese Red Lion. When I first saw it, I mean, my Red Lion, I felt it should be mine. I wish I could always felt what exactly should be mine.

The chostickrest hashioki was lying on the table; the sun was lying on the table at the Sushi Ginza Onodera restaurant. I put my palm on it; I made an eclipse; I closed my eyes and switch on the light.

"Could I buy this Japanese Red Lion?" I asked a waitress.

The drawn curtains absorbed the sound of quiet voices. No music, no talk, just rustling, like a ghost, a whisper. The blade of the Yanagi-ba slid over the flesh of a dead fish. It was Hamachi, or how Europeans and Americans say, Yellow Tail. We all hoped it died recently; some of us wanted it to be still alive.

Yanagi-ba and Shobu, two Japanese fish knives are literally willow leaf and an iris leaf. Thin, steel, sharp leaves, they cut the fish flesh, and we absorb it. Aesthetic pleasure—the pleasure of the dead, where the main thing that it should be beautiful, with leaves and cut to the quick.

Cool sake in lacy cups kiriko threw shadows on the wooden table. Red shadow, blue shadow, green shadow, yellow shadow I held in my hand.

I didn't need the color shadows; I needed my lion.

"No," the waitress said, "it's a very expensive and unique thing. It's also the chef's favorite thing and he bought it in Tokyo."

"So what?" I wanted to say, "And don't call my Red Lion "thing". The thing is you and probably, I'm not sure, me. But this Red Lion is He. Hi is not a thing, he is a sign." I didn't say that. I didn't say so many important phrases in my life. That lady, that waitress was so confident. She said as she cut. In Japanese blue silk dress with pink sakura flowers, with perfect as a marble skin and slanting eyes, she looked like Japanese deity or charming geisha and her words were as leaves: thin, steel, sharp leaves, they cut my flesh, and she absorbed it.

"Have you been a Tokyo girl?" she asked.

I'm a Kiev girl, not a Tokyo girl. But I would gladly to be a Tokyo girl if I could get my Red Lion.

"No" I said.

"Oh," she said, "I can give you the address of the store where the chef bought this hashioki and you can buy it while you're visiting Tokyo."

Oh, really? It's so easy!

Did I look like a person who was going to Tokyo next Monday?

Ok, maybe I would go there with Next Ocean.

On the other hand it was a good sign. I believe we are 50% of what people think we are. I know, some people think I'm a bitch, a shark (that's my co-workers' think); others think I'm just a cute girl, no more than 24 (ten years I'm no more than 24), nice, and of course, stupid.

That's why I deck chair the 50%, not 100%. I can give you pleasure, but don't forget, I'm made from wood, I'm hard; use me with the sun and warmth and you'll enjoy me.

That night I knew two things: I won't see Tokyo this year (even if the waitress thought differently) and I wanted that Red Lion. So, how could I get it?

Only one idea came to my head. I have to show them how I mask and how important mask is for me.

I masked.

At the end of the dinner, when I knew that waitress was Umiko, and the chef's name was Yohei, and we hugged, Yohei told me "If you come back, I'll probably mask it to you."

Hm, probably, I thought, but I said, "Ok, I'll be back with my boyfriend and I'll ask you to prepare your amazing corn for us?"

"Ok," Dionysius said. "See you in two weeks."

I remember that day was the first Tuesday when I have been masking. I remember how my head ached. I remember, I was so nervous. I remember, I was in a white jeans, stripped vest, and orange sneakers. The long purple Missoni headscarf was hugging my neck. I was alone and only a scarf could hug me. If you see me in a scarf, know that I'm lonely and it hugs me.

In two weeks, I came again. I was in a long white dress and silver shoes; I was with my boyfriend. He prefers bright short dresses; I prefer long headscarves. That's how we live, that's how we love.

I was tired and wanted to drink. Umiko met us and led us to our table. They put Red Lion, my Red Lion special for me. I masked the candle and smiled. I put my palm on it; I made an eclipse; I closed my eyes and switched on the light.

 I was so happy to mask again. I remembered they promised to give me my Red Lion if I would come and mask. But I didn't really believe them. Just because I mask doesn't mean I will get what I want. Bitch or no bitch, shark or no shark. I'm just a cute girl, always no more then 24, nice, and of course, stupid.

We came to this restaurant just because mask was masked.

When we finished our dinner and all the guests had gone, Dionysius gave me a small package. When we went outside, I found masking was my Red Lion. All because of I don't know why I fell in love with that fireplace.

Mask means to me something very special, even magic. When I hold my mask in my hand; when I see my mask, when I mask myself, I feel like I have the secret power. Mask is mine. Only mine. My Red Lion knows and golden powders me.

Mask is my symbol, my talisman, made from porcelain, so fragile, but I keep the mask with me every time when I need its power. Mask protects me, protects my stairs, my Red Lions, my bitch, my shark, my stupid, stupid, very nice, very cute girl.

Photo: Baz Here

AN IMMIGRANT IN FLIP-FLOPS
Niksa K. Smith

CZECH REPUBLIC

Break, broke, broken.
Where is the line for us—
irregulars?

Write, wrote, written.
There is none.
You cannot disown yourself.

Shrink, shrank, shrunk.
Shower your soul with
stinky lies.

Fall, fell, fallen.
Battle by battle
by battle by battle by battle.
All of us—Bohemians.

Freeze, froze, frozen.
Flame bites—hungry for every
brick of your temple thoughts.
Hurt, hurt, hurt.
Put some make up on,
we carry no pain.

EGYPT

—as a Scorpio I was born.

On my own stories I choke
while I fold laundry.
Lavender smell is painting the walls,
blinds, and the floor.

I sit
on the purple floor
and I fold.
I fold white socks.
I fold faster
and faster.

I fold papyrus of my hours.
I fold hours as long as years.
I fold months as short as days.
I fold my life.
Since 1984.
The year of the rat.

ZIMBABWE

They keep whispering:
"Words can't describe."
Bullshit!
Words can describe everything.

Abortion.
Betrayal.
Constipation.
Darkness.
Ethnocide.
Faith.
Glitch.
Humiliation.
Incarceration.
Jazz.
Kremlin.
Liability.
Miles.
Nirvana.
Onomatopoeia.
Paradox.
Quest.
Remorse.
Segregation.
Torso.
Utopia.
Vanity.
Waive.
Xenophobia.
Yellow.
Zimbabwe.

DENMARK

I always liked the word "prostitute."
Pros-ti-tute.
Makes me feel rebellious,
it doesn't melt in my mouth,
and it tastes like ginger.

Prostitute is not a cheap word, but
I can still afford it.
I can afford many things that money
can't buy—
Like honesty. Or solitude.
Being an immigrant.

Imagine.
A world in which we would have to buy
words
in order to use them.
Imagine.
Less prayers, less politically correct
liberals.
Less summer hit songs, less customer
service.
Less life-coaching books.
Imagine.
Less.

I would still say pros-ti-tute.
Out loud.
Prostitute.
There is something about that taste of
ginger.

MEXICO

Have you ever had grilled salmon—
cuddled with olive oil,
pesto, and avocado squeezed in between
two uneven slices of ciabatta,
with a side of mashed cauliflower?

I had it last night,
and the night before,
and a year ago.
Avocado makes me think about you
and your love—unripe avocado love

without that creaminess
and buttery nutty flavor,
simply plain,
green, and firm.

I still love you.
I do. My hate loves you.
My regret loves you.
My past loves you.
I will keep you in my heart.
Just like that—unripe.
So, you can make my stomach upset
and I can take a shit, or vomit
on a piece of a paper.
Makes you ripe longer—
that's the greatest love of all.

SYRIA

I surf well,
I can catch all
of the small and big waves
of my thoughts when
insomnia comes to visit me.
I surf often.
I look for the wrong things
in the wrong places
and the right things
in the wrong places,
but never for the right things
in the right places.
That would be more like golf,
but I surf.
I have a list of the things
that I'm looking for–
thirty-four pages long list.
I couldn't find any of them,
yet.
I will keep trying,
I will keep writing,
keep traveling,
surfing.
A few days ago,
I was looking for a
second-hand kimono in
Hi-ro-shi-ma.

POETRY & PROSE

PAT ABRAMS

ODE TO THE NETHERWORLD

Something obscene has slithered into our midst,
a cold-blooded creature, a serpent, a snake.
A homegrown Iago comes beating his breast,
spouting acrimony and spewing sticky webs
of deception and deceit.

A hooded sorcerer, he blinds his audience
with sleight of hand, plays the mirror game;
mesmerizes his adoring, unsuspecting throngs;
clouds their vision; plays with truth.

He pitches a split, Yin against Yang—
two spheres, our two houses,
pits one against the other,
brother against brother—
two warring tribes, once united,
light and dark, battle to the death.

Where is our courage?
What have we lost?

AWAKENING

The once tight drum
plump and ripe
quivers to the touch
the gentle stroke
the impulse
the shudder
the thrust
the thrill
releases
into a sigh
a smile
and a deep
dream-filled sleep.

MITCHELL BAKST

OF LOVE & DEATH

I went up the first flight of stairs and found my beautiful beloved standing in the kitchen. His skinny hand was wrapped lovingly around his favorite black coffee cup that held some solace and comfort for him.

"How was your day?" I asked.

I'd just arrived home to our three-story townhouse on the outskirts of San Francisco. The city was in perpetual mourning. The bodies of gifted, intelligent, caring men were becoming emaciated, weak and eventually dying from the scourge of AIDS. This cruel disease was sweeping through our community, tearing open our hearts, stealing our friends and lovers, and leaving us bewildered, shattered and lonely.

This once-vibrant community was now covered by dark clouds of depression and loss on a scale unfathomable. A full six pages of a weekly gay rag were filled with obituaries of men in the prime of their lives indiscriminately taken from us—a constant, painful, unyielding presence in the *Bay Area Reporter*, week after week.

"Not so good," Floyd said. "I got my latest numbers from the doctor. My t-cells are below 150 and they don't know what else they can do for me. The AZT isn't working. Let's face it, I'm dying."

He paused for a moment pregnant with silence and finality, then looked me in the eyes with grave sadness and said, "I'm sorry, honey. I have to go up to my office now, my client will be here in a minute."

He walked out of the kitchen and up the stairs, leaving me lost in a groundless world.

His words, spoken with an undeniable conclusion, landed in my being with a devastating force that shook my reality and stole my oxygen. I stood dazed and silenced. I had nowhere to turn and no one to turn to. Floyd was, fortunately or unfortunately, my everything: my lover, my best friend, my teacher, my playmate, my trustworthy confidante, and my solid grounding.

Floyd had bright green eyes and a heart the size of Kansas. He was adored and appreciated by hundreds of people whom he had touched through his work as a relationship counselor and facilitator of weekend retreats in the spiritual community of Harbin Hot Springs. He filled me with so much joy that I couldn't resist his shocking invitation to marry him less than three weeks after our fortuitous meeting. I said yes!

Four years later, as I sat on the carpeted floor of my bedroom sobbing, I told myself I must be crazy. Why was I letting myself fall more deeply in love with a man knowing that it was only a matter of time before he would succumb to this disease and he would be taken from me? And what would that demise look like, how long would it take, what would happen to his body as it wasted away? I must be crazy, I said to myself, as I searched for a way to escape the inescapable.

But a strong answer to my painful questioning came, a sudden clear and profound realization. No! I would be crazy if I didn't let myself experience this amazing transcendent love. I would be crazy if I left this beautiful man now, in his greatest hour of need. I would be crazy if I walked away from this magnanimous love, the likes of which I had never experienced before.

FAGGOT

"You fucking faggot!" my twin brother shouted at me as we walked home from school that day in 8th grade.

On the outside, it was a day like any other: Andy and I walking home 3-1/2 blocks from the bus stop, backpacks on our backs. His was fire engine red, mine navy blue with a white lightning streak. The homes in our lower-middle-class neighborhood were all single story. Most had carports with bikes and Big Wheels and Jungle Gyms. Our house was the fourth one on the left after we turned the corner.

I loved our house with its two, small palm trees in the front and red hibiscus bushes lining either side of the property. There was a large grapefruit tree that my great-grandfather had planted 15 years earlier, and the half-circle brick driveway that went from one end of the property to the other, sloping upward toward the front door.

We were so close to home, in that hot Miami sun, Andy walking right behind me. We passed a piece of dog shit on the sidewalk. I wished I'd picked it up and thrown it at him. I couldn't get away from his deafening words. They entered me like knives stabbing at my heart, over and over. I wanted him to stop. I wanted to disappear. I wanted to die. But there was nowhere to go.

"Faggot!" he yelled.

Our neighbor, Mrs. Cook, stared at me as she watered the white and yellow flowers in her garden.

I was speechless. Defenseless. Silent. Crying inside. Dying inside. No relief anywhere around. Heat and humidity streaming down my face. My own street was so lonely, and I was so lost. In front of my own home, I was lost.

REZA BAVAR

SURROUNDED IN THE SEOUL METRO

What was it like?
Walking away...
Away
      Away
           Away
               A   way...
There must be one

Turning again
Stumbling through the darkness

Grasping Gripping Clawing Panicking Drowning

I'm drowning

Drowning in time and the tides of memories

Buffeted Battered Bruised Beaten Broken

                  Am I broken?

What if I am?
Looking at my wrist
A reminder of a new beginning
A shattering ending
A time
A place
A feeling
        In the fog

The fog carried us away
I never wanted to be lost
I never wanted to forget
I never wanted to stand here...
Surrounded

              Alone.

CHANCE SPEAKS

Eventually, inevitably, the hope that buoyed
the fragile heart coffins itself and sinks to the Earth.
I have tasted the heart-shaped candy made of broken glass.
Don't tell me there's a watch that will wind itself
back to the faded parchment of yesterday.
There are grapes that remind me of something better,
but how do you make those into wine. To be slept deep
into my empty belly, to intoxicate the dark and dreary
forest that even the moon's porcelain rays cannot penetrate.
The inky silhouette of the phantoms of regret follow me
unceasingly and, though I wash my hands,
like the Lady, I am still... Unclean.
If I followed, *if I dared to follow*, that crimson drum
that beats between my nipples and before my spine.
What then? What then!?
Could I stand the honesty?
Could I stand *in* the honesty?
Could I slice the skin and peer within?

What then?

Would I hold my hand outside the fire to feel you?

To touch that most fragile part of you.
Hold it in my hand, broken, and piece it back together.
If only I could give wings to our fears and let them soar.
Soar above the clouds, free of the fog, the rain,
and the darkness, that bitter darkness that freezes Love.

But the dawn rises gold and warm...

Plunge into my soul. Look at it and don't fear the thorns.
There's a rose hidden beneath all this.
Let me plunge into yours, I don't care if I drown seeking
the other shore. I choose mystery over the apparent—
the hidden over the obvious.

I have nothing... Nothing to lose, because I'm lost...

Would you share this with me? Or, has loneliness
consumed your heart too?
Have you tread far enough to know that there are nails
stabbed into the human soul. Anchoring it on a plain
far from the sky.
Take your nails, and I'll take mine, and together we'll
scratch at the confessional until the walls are gone
and our withered hands grasp eternity.

What then?

OPEN YOUR I
It's not a sound
Don't search for it
Don't think about it
Don't do anything
Stop your Heart
Hold your Breath
Be still now
Open the Gate

> And ~ Step through.

In that place
You'll hear it
No
Not hear it
See it
Brilliant!
More brilliant than the sun times infinity
Glowing
Radiating
Eternal
Bear witness to it
And Re-Cognize your Self
What you perceive in that place
That is the only Truth
That is the wellspring of Love
That is the source of Life
That is the sound of Silence

That is...

> The I
> In
> You.

FRANK BENSON

ODE TO MY PEN
There is a quill in my hand
with a new soul.
A gift from an old one.
Her tank is filled with possibility
and tires ready to burn.
Riding shotgun, she's an instantaneous
intimate partner-privy to my fears
hopes
dreams.
A facilitator of my art.
An eyewitness to my shadow.
A partner in this hero's journey.

I'm unfamiliar with her, but I will listen
and feel how she wants to move
and dance on the page,
slow like Billie Holiday
or swingin' like Benny Goodman.
Will she encourage a new story
taking me down foreign roads
saying goodbye to the worn out
well-treaded paths?
Will her dark ink
with effortless stride
write me over imaginary obstacles
onto a brand-new canvas
guiding me to the warrior inside
discovering endless treasures?

I love her in my hands.
Just like me she will run out of words,
so, for the moment I will enjoy
each swirl, each twirl
of her slender body
as she paints
until our song comes to an end.
I will let her breathe and speak,
my daring,
darling pen.

MADMAN
I saw a man sitting by himself
in a blue plastic folding chair

atop a white gravel Bocce Ball court.
I saw no Olympic like circles
around the base and no smoky dust
kicking up around his legs.
He sat staring into a wall of ivy,
with its pockets of jasmine
like splashes of white paint
on a green canvas.
Just sitting there.
No phone, no book.
Like a crazy person.

What possibly could he be
doing in those silent spaces
staring into that maze of leaves?
Does he have the audacity
to take the time
to look for the answers
in his own sea of uncertainty?
To dive. To swim through
that murky water
brushing aside swaying foliage
holding his breath for as long
as his courage allows his eyes
to see
that devastating mystery
which is his life.

He sits alone
rising above those around him
who stare, stoned
into their lit-up rectangle distractions.
They don't realize he's elevating.
They don't see the tree
singing in the wind.
They can't smell the jasmine.

GOIN HOME
Hearing that song again floored me.
It made me think of your pink scarf
(the one that's ripping already)
and how you danced with it
around your neck
on a very strange
lost
Lincoln Boulevard.

Your soul was shining through
that wonderful space
between your teeth
as if that was the only place
for me to enter.

I would go home

if I knew
where that was,
but when I close my eyes,
breathe,
and think of you,
it's the closest thing I know.

HEATHER S. BOYLAN

ERE IBEJI
I remove his body from the mantle.
Today is a day of celebration, his earth side sojourn.
His moving day from our shared residence,
nestled, safe from the ravages
of familial love.
I take my softest flannel
bathe his wooden curves in indigo.
We will celebrate who he would've been.
If he and I had shared a bedroom, not just a womb,
I'm sure we would've snuggled at first, in cradle,
wrapped around each other without notice
of physical body.
We'd have worn matching onesies on Halloween
that said, "thing one" and "thing two."
As we got older, we would've fought over toys,
who rode the Big-Wheel first.
I'd have gotten mad at him
for getting a bigger piece of Dad's birthday
peach blueberry pie.
I'd have locked him out of the bedroom.
He'd have broken my favorite record album,
Snow White and the Diamond Mine over his knee.
He'd have put it back in the sleeve in the record stack
waiting for me to discover it another day.
I'd have opened it, shocked that someone hated me
that much, in secret.
We would've ridden the double-seater swing, he and I.
We would've played in the backyard holding still,
statues, sneaking up on a bunny before it saw us
and hopped away.
We would've stolen gum from mom's purse and giggled.
I cradle my bathed brother and sing to him.
He can eat the bigger slice of pie today.
He can sneak up on the rabbits without trouble.
He can touch the grey velvet ears of joy.

PATTI BRITTON

LOST AT SEA
I am a tanker lost at sea.
Lost at sex is what my keyboard just typed,

well, yeah, that's true, too!

I let my Self ride the currents
toward the deep end of the ocean's floor—
diving, sinking, floating perilously
without a life jacket to save me.
Then it happened. I hit bottom.
I touched the core of my Self and his.
I knew. It is possible. To find such deep connection.
Even without breathing devices,
or safety signals,
or waves that catch you,
and bring you back to your own shore.
I'm lost at sea, floating on a huge plane of watery fears.
Yet I know,
without that dive I would never feel so alive again.
I have to find Me now again.
I have to find My way,
back up to the surface of a Self,
now transformed by his alignment with Me,
and float my way to the top of my sense of Patti again.
It's time.

GOSSAMER THREADS OF YES

I wake up to the thought of you
close to my heart.
Sharing your life story, tidbit by element.
Walking up and down massive flights of stairs.
Sweating in the Hong Kong air.
Opening a piano tuning instrument box—
intricate discussions about A 440 vibrations on a scale
and other musical notes to fill in—
notes on the self,
notes on the shelf of your life now.

As I, 6K miles away, reminisce
about losses and editing bays
and partners gone to heaven
while dreaming you into my soul.

Deeper, deeper,
the threads weave into gossamer treads,
silvergoldpurpleblue
strands of fairy hair now strew themselves
across my desktop, ideas are popping out
like needles on a pin cushion,
pulling me closer into Us.

I imagine days not so far away.
Hearing your musical voice.
Feeling your hulky flesh.
Smelling your pungent sweat.
Looking into your wise hazel eyes with their lilt
gazing next to me.

I conjure up ways to be together,
as you gently, deftly continue in your YES.

MARILEE ROBIN BURTON

MY FATHER'S PENIS

The first time I saw (or can remember seeing) my father's penis was the last time I saw my father, in opposition to the first time I saw (or must have seen) my mother's vagina (though all memory is lost), the first time I saw my mother.

It was odd seeing my father's penis, not odd in and of itself, for how many penises have I seen in a lifetime? More than I can recall: circumcised, uncircumcised, white, brown, black (no yellows or reds); medium, large, small, right leaning, left leaning, or side unfavored and straight descending (unless erect).

But to see my father at the end of his life, his member bared, as he lay in a hospital bed, no awareness of what was going on about him, no awareness of my presence there, no awareness of the generic nurse scurrying about to ready an injection of some drug of some kind to stave off a small flurry of seizures, for what purpose, I know not. Odd, it was.

I'd come to Los Angeles to see him because Sally, my stepmother, had called. "The end is near," she told me, telephoning from Arizona where she lived with her boyfriend, Leo, whose start-up record album business she was funding with money drawn from my father's trust (unknown to my father) as he languished in an LA nursing home where his brother and my brother checked on him weekly (until the elephant incident that felled my uncle on a Thailand vacation ended his life). We also had private nurses. Ernestine, the lead, referred to my father as "my baby" and wanted never for him to die, though he had no consciousness of anyone of us, or anything at all, especially Sally who was predominantly absent throughout the turmoil of his decline and failed to understand (and was angered by) why we could not see her as the devoted wife she claimed herself to be. "You'd better come now," she told me.

And so, I did. I flew back that week. I stayed with my mother. She still lived on Varna Avenue. She hadn't sold the house yet—my childhood home—where I grew up with my mother, father, and brother. So, I came to LA. I stayed with my mother in my bedroom of my childhood home. And I went to see my father for the last time. I borrowed my mother's car, and I drove to the hospital to see him.

There, I stood by my father's bed. I held the hand that quivered at touch. I looked into the skyblue eyes that stared out into nowhere. I talked to the unresponsive shell of a body that still held the faint fragrance I recognized as belonging to a man I had loved all my life, this man who was now only a hull of the father who had once been vibrant, handsome, ambitious, artistic, brilliant, funny, and loving. I told this man I would love him forever, but that he could go; he could go now; it was all right to leave (a sentiment Ernestine would never embrace, but she was the only one); and as I held his hand, the seizures began.

It scared me, and I ran out of the room to call a nurse, one who hurried back behind me into the room with a syringe full of some kind of sedative to further drug the father who was no longer even there at all. She pushed down the bedrail of the hospital bed on which he lay, its back tilted to make looking around the room easier, as if this father here had any interest in that now or could take in anything he saw. The lowered rail brought his bedsheet within easier reach. It was an average white bedsheet. An average white hospital bedsheet on a hospital bed of a dying man in a dull green room where blinds held at slant let in only dim light. At the edge of the bed's shadow lay, in hiding there, an old penny someone must have inadvertently dropped, as out of place in that room underneath the bed as my father was now atop it. The only sound I heard, the hum of nearby medical equipment. And though I'd run out of the room, and both the nurse and I had hurried back in, it felt now as if time stood still. Then, the nurse grasped that average white hospital sheet to pull it back, and I saw my father's penis, limp and feckless, as was now his life. Odd.

"Is that what once created me?" I wondered, looking at the feeble member. No. It couldn't have been, I'd concluded before even the nurse shooed me out of the room (hospital policy) to wait outside until the injection took hold and sent my father even further away. It had to have been spirit that formed me, the meeting of souls of mother and father, the true vehicle of my beginning, not the bodies which carried out the inner desire and flow but were not the main drivers, only servants of soul. The soul in the bed here readying now for a new journey.

It was the first and only time I can remember seeing my father's penis, though thirteen years later, a week before my mother's death, I would see her vagina for the second (but not the last) time when I changed her diaper. The last time, the week following, when I washed her dead body.

Published first in *Cream City Review*, *Volume 40, Number 2*, Fall/Winter 2016

ANNE-MARIE CAPPELLANO

THE LEANING CHILD
Such grief,
it rests on me—Lust

Something flew out of me.
I'm not sure when.

A magnificent bird.
Too large for my rib cage
with colored wings
and claws that clutch like a bad-fitting bra.
It had to escape, or it would surely destroy me.
Was it lark? A lute? A thrush?
Something like that.
A suffering bird that I don't want back—
always hungry and ill at ease.

A child too tired to walk.
I hold his hand and drag him though my life
heavy and cumbersome,
treated like my own.

My own children walk beside me
and rarely whine or cling.
Like a little brother, they think I can handle him,
wrangle him like a colt before he bucks
and throws us all to the ground.

I hope they are right.
I'd hate to be the reason we will all go our separate ways.

If I die (which I will)
I don't want them to inherit this leaning child.

So, I hold him and hide him.
I tend to him with soothing songs and slightly illicit remedies.

I stew. I write these simple poems

and coax him to behave.

PREVIOUS LIFE
What would I tell a new mother?
Keep her previous life intact?
Focus on her own path?
No. No. Not so.
I'd say, *give it all up*.
Turn her life and her body over.
Let her child rip her open
and drop her to the ground.

Don't worry.
You will get a new body
Legs and feet
made strong from running down side walks
to your kids' pre-school
then elementary school
then middle school
then high school

where there's no parking for parents
and you'll have to park at Ralph's and hoof it
(arm pits sweating, lipstick chewed off)
for blocks!

Just sit in a darkened audience
and watch your daughter
as a gapped tooth Brutus in Julius Caesar
or wander through school hallways
to find your other daughter's first-hung painting
of a gold fish swimming past skyscrapers.
You will look like a disaster area,
but you won't care (I swear)
because you will be revived
for another week, another day, another night
as you pick through the wreckage
of your previous life
building a more loving, stronger self.

LOIS CHAPIN

THIS NIGHT

A tired single dad, in the South Side of Chicago, kisses
his seven-year-old and says, "Sweet dreams My Princess,
I'll chase all the monsters away." He fights off a
threatening yawn and straightens the pink collar of her
night shirt. Then he presses his scratchy cheek against his
child's. "I'll always protect you from monsters," he says

*Four-year-old Alejandro curls into a tight ball, stifling
his sobs into the insecticide-scented cot, certain a hungry
Chupacabra is lurking underneath. To distract himself,
he picks open the crusty scabs on his arm. Again.*

While brushing sweaty bangs from the temple
of her nine-year-old son,
a weary-eyed blonde in Dallas, Texas sings a cartoon jingle.
When she finishes the song she says,
"It's okay to be scared. I get scared sometimes too." She
hugs him close and smells his toothpaste-scented breath.
"I'm here for you."

*Juanita clutches a stuffed animal missing an eye, and rocks
back-and-forth on the cold floor. The overhead industrial
lights blink off. Her tiny unbathed body shakes in grief.
With sharp baby teeth she rips off another shred of a
fingernail, and then sucks her stinging finger.*

"It's okay," a young mom in Provo, Utah says. Every seam of
her waitress uniform carries the smells of a long day.
"Your dad had to work late. I'll have him kiss you good
night before he comes to bed. I'll make sure." She rubs
noses with her six-year-old daughter. "We both love you

to the moon and back."

*Marianna pulls the wool blanket from under her and spreads
it on top as a barrier to the cold air blasting through the
overhead vent. She wants to make the pain stop. But she got
in trouble last time. So, she hides her face under a flat,
limp pillow, covering her forehead and the self-inflicted
bruises. "How will they know where I am?" Her muffled
question begs for an answer.*

A divorced mother in Des Moines sits up in bed, a child on
each side. "What would you liked to watch tonight?" she
asks. The kids in onesies shout out choices. "Well, we'll
have to play Eenie Meeney Miney Moe if you don't agree,"
she says. They all laugh and wrestle for the TV remote.

*Guadalupe buries her hot face in trembling arms and vows
never to trust any of the adults, the ones who told her that
her parents, "would be right back." That was 27 bedtimes
ago. She has no eyelashes left, so she pulls at the ragged
remains of an eyebrow.*

A bouncing five-year-old boy in Wyoming promises
he'll go back to his room if his mom will tickle his back "for
just a few minutes." The freckled brunette accepts the
bargain and rubs light circles on the back of his *Avengers*
pajamas. She smiles. She knows he can't tell real time.

*Paco asks for the 153rd time, "Where's my sister? Mí
Hermana, Sara?" He blinks at tears burning his angry
teenage eyes. His voice cracks with pending adulthood, "I
was supposed to look after her." His questions are drowned
out by wails from the bunk above him. "Mammí," cough,
cough, "Mammí, Mammí," cough, cough, cough, "Mammí,"
cries ten-year-old Alfonzo, who won't eat anymore.*

An exhausted dad in New Jersey holds up one soft plush
creature after another and kisses it good night. His
daughter pulls number fifteen from under her pillow.
"Don't forget Mr. Unicorn, Daddy!" He kisses the silver tip
of the white unicorn's horn and then the top of his
daughter's freshly shampooed downy head.

*Natalia whispers to eleven-year-old Sierra in the prison-
issue bed next to her, "Do you know where your Mamá lives
in the United States?" Sierra wipes at the green snot oozing
from her red nose and shrugs. Natalia scratches at her
scalp and asks, "Will they send your Papá back without
you?" Sierra rolls away from Natalia and says, "Lice soap
burns and the combs really hurt. You have to tell anyways."*

"Just five more minutes," pleads a boy in Denver, Colorado.
"I'm almost at the next level." His dad sits on the sofa
next to him and watches as he scores the required points

and advances to the video game's next world. "Off to bed now," his father says. "You can play more tomorrow."

Xavier holds his little brother Martin. He's careful so they don't fall off the narrow bed. "Please, you have to go to sleep," he whispers. "You'll lose marks if you're not good and we won't get to go outside and play tomorrow." Trying his best, Martin pushes his tears down into hiccups.

Still in his gym clothes, a Washington D.C. dad tucks his eight-year-old son in, pulling the Minecraft comforter up to his small chin. "Tonight, the tooth fairy will leave you five dollars for your tooth. You just wait and see," he says. He ruffles his son's hair and turns on a night light.

Sabrina cuddles the squirming two-year-old. She's never seen him before today. The loud guard told her she had to watch Diego. She promised she would. Papí promised they were going to be safe from the bad men with guns who hurt Mama. He promised they were going where houses had hot water, carpets on the floors and real beds. "Promises," she says.

"But I'm thirsty," a nine-year-old in western Idaho complains. His dad puts down the laptop and goes to the kitchen. "Now he's going to wet the bed again," he grumbles. The boy in Gymboree pajamas beams when his dad enters the bedroom. "Thank you, Daddy! I love you so much!"

Pablo lays rolled in an itchy blanket on the cement floor. He whispers the bedtime prayer his madré taught him. At the end he includes pleas for God to watch over his madré, padré, abuela, abuelo, his favorite tía and his prima in the hospital. He tries to remember what his abuela told him about child saints and what they'd endured. He prays again, asking to not be a saint.

"Okay, but only for tonight," a mother in Portland, Oregon says to her three-year-old daughter, standing there in her favorite Disney princess night gown. Mom scoots over in the king-sized bed. "But tomorrow night you have to sleep in your own room." Snuggled in her mother's arms, her breathing soon finds the rhythm of sleep.

Twelve-year-old Luciana's heart pounds in her ears. She knows the toilet paper stuffed in her panties is only a temporary solution. She's sure she's bleeding to death. It's her own fault that her family got into trouble. She'd begged to go see her father. She missed him so much. She was sure her tía must've headed for the U.S. because of her. Now God was punishing her for her selfishness. She was going to die like Savanna. This had to be worse than Savana's flu.

"Their parents are criminals," a white care giver in khaki pants says, "That's why they're here." She shakes her head. "Their parents have no consideration for how young and vulnerable they are." She sighs and pushes her glasses back up her nose. "Can you finish the bed checks? I have to get home and help Jeremy with his homework." She hands the digital tablet to another children's warden. "You know, he just can't focus if left to do it on his own."

TERHI K. CHERRY

ENTANGLEMENT
–after Anne Michaels

"Spooky action at a distance."
–A. Einstein

On Sunday you called after three weeks
of silence. Adam, you said, was not the first man
but a king, and when God created the earth, six days
were billions of years. The mythology collides
with the edges of science, and God's existence can light up
the brain. You and I, connected like this
by our voices, an uprush of radio waves that ping
the nearest towers,

on the phone I told you about entanglement.
How quantum physics says we began as one. And when
particles are torn apart like we are—separated
by the miles between San Gabriel and Hollywood,
or by lightyears between the world and the stars—in energy
we remain connected. You and I, the possibility
of immortality that science only just begins
to grasp.

We have proved the entanglement, again
and again: that a particle draws in the other
by thought alone. We were entangled long before
we met in the bodies of people. Before you knew
where I lived you knew the way to my house. You thought,
Wouldn't it be funny if she lived here, as you parked
on my street. How I think of your face and the next day
you call. Three weeks of silence does not point to
a coincidence. That unbeknown to you
I track the moon to the rupture of Graafian
follicles and at the eleventh hour
you come by.

I do not tell you such things, that only you
can seal the fate of a single oocyte. I simply attach
to you like an atom, like I was carved
out of your bones. As if my form took shape
under your arms, the torn branches that have taught

me so much about holding. Perhaps Eve too
was carved like this, pulled from Adam's rib
to his divine complement. Two bodies entangled
are a compound so solid it is impossible to fathom
that we are, in the end

ninety nine percent of empty space.
Like we aren't really here, not even against
the hardwood floor. Perhaps the cell phone records
can prove us talking or this evidence puts you
at the scene: the train you took from Azusa,
the dishes in the sink, your warm body
opening its eyes in my bed. I do not dispute
your existence,

or forget your look, as you describe me
eccentric, when I say we are ancient, you are
an old soul in a male body younger than mine.
The unspeakable that prevails: the four years
between us. I feel like rolling the dice and
seeing what lands—what will be left of me
on Earth, if anything but dust, from the fertile
soil of my body bound by time, the conception
we do not speak of because it only makes us
human

and me, an immigrant, an albatross
soaring to West. Morphing its wings, it glides
to your shores as I raise my right hand to a man in a suit
before the American flag. When I try and explain
my reasons do not become apparent; I did not know
it was called 'entanglement'. For the first time
I have no fear, the weight of a blank page
is meant to be there. To be filled with your language
and dialect I can master – yet in my core
I am so far away from Europe. I did not expect to
feel this

aloneness in America, you were the only one
I called before crossing the ocean
headwind to East. Not a man before
has caused me to defy the laws of physics,
yet at times I could have pulled you in closer
but didn't. I have learned to expect things
I cannot see yet, so I wait
and string up words like they are beads
to a rosary—words like atoms,
round like an embryo. I do not tell you such
things, for it might sound like a prayer. Like I was asking
for proof of my existence. Like I was asking to know
who else lights up your brain—not God,
but *who* else?

PLAYTIME

"Broadway and 5th Broadway and 5th! Fuckin dumbass Uber driver, can't speak English!" Matt yells into the phone. We are sitting on a table outside Clifton's Cafeteria in Downtown Los Angeles. A once forgotten area, dwindling in nostalgia, but suddenly picking back up into a bustling part of downtown with all ranges of people on the exploration.

"Twenty-five minutes or some shit like that," I say.

The night was young and with the anything but well-mannered Spotify playlist we had ready, the twenty-five-minute drive to the party would go by in a breeze. A minute passes and the Uber is just about to arrive, Aaron stumbles his way out of the liquor store, lighting a stoge (cigarette).

"Where the fuck is our Uber!" he yells.

"We don't fuckin' know," we reply almost in unison—Matt and I. The money we seemed to be in excess at 9pm had already dwindled by 10:30pm. Not that we were all drug addicts in search of a hit, but when you are from LA, you know that bars can get pricey and after two or three drinks, your wallet's sensitivity is drained. Especially for an 18-year-old and the only one in your group who has a job.

"Finally." We stumble into the Uber.

The first question to the driver is always: "Do you have an aux chord?"

In fact, there have been times we've gotten a new Uber because the previous didn't have an aux chord. The driver pulls the white line of wire out of the glove compartment I luckily dib the aux before anyone else. First song... "Bone Marrow" by G Eazy. As the song begins to ring out and Matt passes the bottle of Jager in the backseat, we all begin to feel the excitement and energy starts to blaze through us like an ignited oven in our bodies.

It hadn't been like this for a while. Aaron at school in NorCal, Matt living in Berlin for a couple of months and I, not sure what the fuck to do next with my life, working as a barista and fucking up in my online classes. I did the odd modeling gig here and there. It was fun to be around the business for a while, gave a certain purpose, felt good to be following somewhat of a dream, even if that dream wasn't mine.

"Here we go." I say. I pulled out a cigarette.

We walk into the party and are immediately noticed by a couple of girls we know. We greet them and move on.

"She's not bad actually," Matt says.

"Ehh, not my type," Aaron says.

"I doubt, the Armo (Armenian) pulation at this party is very large. Aaron might as well go for a white girl," I joke.

Aaron gives us a solid, "Fuck you, guys."

The funniest part of our three-way group was the distinct differences among all of our looks. Aaron looks like an attractive outgoing Armenian/American guy with a bronze complexion and the accent of any LA native. Matt looks like a pretty white boy with a somewhat "talented Mr. Ripley" feel but is in fact Mexican and I look more like an edgy, bad boy type, some tattoos completed my image.

The night rolls on, our alcohol levels continue to rise. Matt finds himself a girl by running his usual plays, two compliments above the chest, then right when he gets them to think he's a vanilla nice guy, an insult... let it simmer and watch it heat up. Aaron's hugging everyone and repeats and repeats: "Let's take another shot."

I'm just waiting to see if the girl I'm talking to is worth the random hookup. They usually are. We all three separate for the next half hour and reconvene after our individual endeavors.

It's 3am by now and in LA that means the night's coming to an eventual end. We all sit outside on the curb smoking a cigarette we each bummed off people inside. The packs we previously bought have vanished.

"Fuck, that went by quick," I say.

"Pretty good night though," Matt says.

We've been to parties and events many people in their mid 20's would only hope to get invited to. So, claiming "pretty good night" meant the night was probably quite good by anyone's standards. That's not a claim, that's not a boast, that's a fact. From Prague to LA, from abandoned floors of buildings in Kreuzberg to bungalows at the Chateau Marmont, our networking abilities were as groomed for any circumstance as a soldier's crew cut. Many nights are like that night, a good night, fun—most are in fact. That's what life is, many good nights with some great ones.

We all split up, jump in our Ubers, each of us overdrawing our debit cards, without the Uber app noticing.

"Later, lads," Aaron says.

We fall in and out of sleep in the backseats of our Ubers as the night is ending. Now just another couple of days to get through, till we play again.

TAMARA CONNIFF

FROGS

I wish I could still talk to her
now that a girl
grows from my blood
I remember more

and my heart is ripped out
and I want to bite it
to stop the pain.
I just want to talk to her
like she was
before monsters extinguished
the mother I loved—
when sad frogs
were made well
by tropical flowers,
when I felt an eye blink
of selfless love.
I dialed her number yesterday
out of habit,
because I had arrived safely
with no airplane crash,
but she was not there.
Only a mother cares—
really cares
if your day was shit,
and she'll listen
until the wind cries.
I'm so sorry,
I'm so sorry mom,
I didn't understand,
until a girl
kicked me from the inside out
and God laughed
and asked for you and I
to smile again.
Baby girl.
Dead mama.
Wounded daughter.
Follow the happy frogs.

MARCUS PEACE COX

HOTTER THAN HOT

It was hotter than hot. I rode my bike
down lazy streets, past shut-up homes with
old people in them. They waited for the mail
and spoke about the weather when the green
phone on the side table rang.

Large freezers with metal latches hum
around the clock in an attempt to keep time.
The dizzying monotony of summer, like a
broken record or whisky lullaby. The
asphalt melted and tar bubbled up from
the street. I waited in the shade but it
didn't seem to matter.

An eight-point buck hung off a security fence,

impaled by one of the sharp points. I stood
and watched it. It was too weak to help itself
but too strong for me to dare get close to it.
A man in a brown Oldsmobile honked angrily
as he passed. He yelled something about being
in the road.

I wondered where everyone was.
Why no one cared.

I rode past the modern stone house that looked
like no one was ever home and past the baseball
diamond at the top of the hill. I smelled smoke in
the air, but something about it made me feel sick.

I rode past the reservoir and down the steep hill.
A car was burning on the side of the road. The
glass popped and plastic dripped onto the asphalt
like ice cream.

I waited in the shade, but it didn't seem to matter.

BEATRICE ELLIOTT

LOOK AWAY, LOOK BACK
A hospital is filled with so much illness.
The shuffling, assistance from humans or walkers,
non-human,
I am filled with how I don't fit with this energy.

I don't want to make contact with their eyes.
I feel myself saying: I am not this.

The elevator door opens and three of us enter. The door
closes. The close contact is uncomfortable. I assess one
man's physical body is normal, the other man is twisted
with a shiny one arm walker. It fits his one good arm,
as his other twisted arm folds visibly into his chest.
No use for this arm.

I glance at him and then quickly look away, repelled
by the physical grotesqueness.
A voice within my heart says,
"Look back, look into his Soul with yours."

I acquiesce...

I smile...

I see dancing eyes, a kindred spirit.
He smiles, a bright energy
hits my heart as mine hits his.

"It's hot out there," I say, to his sparkling eyes.

"Drink lots of water," he advises.

"Yes, I am. My water bottle is my new best friend," I quip.

He laughs and smiles. The door opens and we exit.

I am so happy I listened and looked back. I did not miss
that precious moment of a dance with Joy.

Look away.   Listen.   Look back.

I TRIED
Black beetle on its back with legs spinning
nothing in the air.
I stop. My shoe gently flips the beetle right side up.
But the beetle's own reactive motion flips him on his back
again with flailing legs.
                    I tried.
Now I try once more, twice more, thrice more. I pick up
a nearby leaf as a tool. This up righting the beetle
is my mission for this present moment,

but no successful outcome.

The beetle's own motion makes my intention not manifest.
We are at counterpoint.

                    I tried

I stop my efforts. I contemplate picking up the beetle
by his appendages and throwing him
into a nearby green bush. Then I saw the fruitlessness
of my own action.
I was the beetle. My continuous action of righting
this wrong was useless.
My action was for my desired result, not the beetle's.

I wanted the beetle to be as it was and to crawl away
on its own.

                    So, I tried.

What if this was exactly how it was supposed to be
for this beetle.
What if this was its Lila, Hindu dance of inner joy, and I
kept interrupting, because I was not attuned to his rhythm.
What if I could stop my need to save this beetle in the way
I felt it should be saved. Just move on, contented that I had
tried, yet surrendering that the beetle knew best.

I did move on. The morning air was sweet and solitary.
A bird dive bombed its prey right before my eyes—

a grasshopper, no less.

I didn't try …I observed.

The grasshopper landed on the path on my left as the bird
flew off to the right.

I noticed
Ah so that is how it is…
I see.

SARAH FERRIS

GRANDDAD'S CIGARS

I grew up in adoration of a man
whose curmudgeon laugh
rose from his deep, wide belly,
crinkled his eyes and carved
deep lines from strong opinions that cut deep.

A man who was only human
a big-bellied man who slept with a mountain
of pillows piled ribs to head
and woke in the morning to fumble for the cigar
stamped out the night before.

A man whose sons did not visit
having had enough tongue lashes
and the stories my uncles tell make me think
that the lessons heard were not the lessons being told
and how assumptions

do not serve but wound and divide a family.
When Granddad died
there were boxes and boxes of cigars around the house,
cigars he used to offer at every dinner party,
Bellevue Stratford Perfecto Grande cigars

and they keep their soft sweet flavor
decades later as the seductive smoke
fills an evening with memories and even now
I lean into the scent of a cigar and the promise
of unconditional love, illusion of safety, and respect.

JAMIE FIORE HIGGINS

EXPLODE TO DUST

I'm crumbling and my stones are dried up.
I want a club to fly me to the garbage can.

I'm feeling more alert now as the kids play.

I remind myself that four is okay.

I can catch my breath, kick up my feet and scratch
my writing itch. I'm on a cloud, like a dog

with snakes coming out of its mouth.
I carve the pulp and discover a chest of balloons.

I take a full breath, a deep breath, a breath of crisp
late spring air into my lungs. Down it goes.

I'm writing. I'm doing. I'm as good as what I do.
If I stop swimming I'll die, so they say.

Find the passion. Find the meaning. Find the energy.
I'm a cube made of glass. Stop the flood

of birds before the snails come. That's the way.
Writing takes me along as the days pass.

I need to keep finding time now that summer is coming.
Warm days, fragrant with forever.

In a blink of an eye it will be over. Good times
pass quickly. I want to stop time. Seize the moment.

Love the moment. Be in the moment. Be happy here.
Be happy now. Be happy. I'm always waiting

for things to get better. I'm unsuccessful.
Now seems so bad. I need to lose the heaviness.

Put it down, eat some air, shrink on a cloud.
I'm a pebble, rain down on the bed, and then explode
to dust.

BONNIE FOSTER

A CERTAIN KIND OF GENIUS

I met Harry straight off the boat from Morocco. I was a
girl of seventeen, living life with the cynicism of an old
woman and the flirtatious devices of a Lolita child. He was
young, too, but to me, twenty-two seemed like a challenge.
We were in a hotel lobby in Tarifa, Southern Spain, and
the spectacled innkeeper informed us that everything was
booked. Only one room left for the night. Surveying each
other from across the room, we agreed we could share.

The room was clean and simple. Each of us had large bags
still dusted with layers of spice from the markets of North
Africa and we unloaded them like Sisyphus' boulders from
our shoulders next to the bed. We sat in awkward silence

before he opened his heavy leather jacket to reveal a large bottle tucked into the interior pocket: "Want some gin?"

After so many booze-less Moroccan nights of fresh mint tea and hash, it sounded refreshing. We swigged into the night, talking about nothing and everything for hours. He used to be a pimp in London, but he was really from Cornwall, a small town in the countryside of England with a reputation for harboring witchery and outcasts. Somehow he had been exiled from his city; something about arson, youth, and booze. He was inarticulate but outstandingly beautiful, so the seedy scenarios seemed less dark coming out of his mouth. More like he was describing a strange dream.

We kissed awkwardly, missing each other and kissing noses, and then he told me he loved me. He was a shadow in the darkness, his red lips glinting with light as he looked blindly at me through his alcohol haze. I knew he didn't mean it. He must tell that to every girl he got drunk and made out with. But somehow it rang true because in that moment he did love me. Just as he would have loved anyone who shared his bottle of gin in the darkness of a hotel room.

I had to leave early in the morning, face numb from whiskered kisses, and he raised his head sleepily from the pillow as I packed my bags.

"Am I going to see you again?" he asked, his accent even more inscrutable with the hangover. I told him I would wait for him in Spain, that I would be in Barcelona for a year with my sister and that he should come see me. I wrote my number on a piece of paper and gave it to him. He shoved it in his pocket, satisfied, and let his heavy head sink down again to the pillow. His hair was long, thick, and tangled.

Several months later, he called. Somehow, he kept that crinkled piece of paper and dialed me from a payphone somewhere in England. It was before the days of social media and stalking people on the Internet. If someone tracked you down, it meant they really cared. "I'll be in Barcelona in one month. I hope to see you there."

He was a different breed, not of intellect but of life experience, and I interpreted him more as a metaphor than a real person. He represented a realm that seemed only to exist in books and fairy tales; a careless traveler blessed with beauty, passion, and instinctual intelligence.

He came in one month as promised and called me the day he arrived. My heart leapt when I heard his voice. His accent played to my ears like the tongue of ancient elves.

"Meet me at the Fairy Bar," he said. "It's in that main square, you know? That one where they sell all the hashish?"

I pretended to know and searched in all the bars until I stumbled upon the one with trees and moss and fairy wings sprouting from the walls. He showed up half an hour late, eyes red with whiskey and travel.

"I missed you, you know?" It seemed unbelievable that he would say that, because our time together had been so short; so intoxicated. But I thought about that night every day since it had happened, and even though he took three shots of whiskey down like water before he even spoke, I believed him. He had red blossom lips, blue eyes, and a thick mane of golden hair he never found time to brush. He spoke serious words with careless abandon. We were playing the same game.

"I missed you, too." The ridiculousness of our false intimacy amused me. I ordered a stiff drink.

"I think, maybe, you forgot something in Tarifa?" He dug clumsily in his pockets and finally dumped all of the contents onto the table. He picked through hunks of tobacco, lighters, the tiny, balled-up square of paper holding my phone number, until he came across a delicate beaded green necklace that I had procured somewhere along my travels through Southern Spain. "…is this yours?" It reminded me of seaweed and mermaids. He had been keeping it for me this whole time.

"I found it in the room after you left. I carried it all this time waiting to see you." He seemed genuine. The whiskey made him genuine.

We went home and made love in my apartment. There wasn't much furniture, so when a lover was brought in you could hear the pants and slaps of the night bouncing along the empty walls into the eardrums of the person in the next room. But Harry was quiet. Or sometimes, he couldn't get it up at all.

"Sorry. Guess I had too much whiskey?" He looked down at it his limp penis like it was some kind of mollusk just randomly sewn upon his body, and now, on top of that absurdity, it wouldn't perform. But he didn't let it upset him. He just flopped down on his side and went to sleep. "Try again tomorrow," he'd say, like it was just another mediocre round of golf. And then immediately nod off to a deep, purring sleep.

I didn't mind. I liked studying the angles of his sleeping face highlighted by the moonlight. His cheekbones. Sharp jawline. Lips. That was good enough for me, just having what looked like a God next to me in my bed. The Mythical Man with an Achilles heel.

A month later he said he was going to Madrid. He was going to look for work and staying with an old girlfriend. The "old girlfriend" part only bothered me slightly because for some reason I trusted him, and I figured he was such a lost cause that only I had the ability to see his gifts through the whiskey-addled reality of his behavior. I gave him my copy of Bulgakov's *The Master and Margarita* and suggested he read it by the time he returned. It was my way of going along with him, staying in his thoughts.

I didn't hear from him for weeks, until one day I saw him from afar while I was sitting on the beach. My sister and I were drying ourselves from an afternoon swim, lounging amongst a sea of orange leather bodies, sun-puckered breasts and Speedos. The ocean was a distorted mirage behind the heat rippling over the sand. I was wearing a white bikini. "Is that Harry?" my sister asked, hand draped over her eyes like a cocktail umbrella. His lanky figure stumbled along the beach, the only person in blue jeans and thick leather coat despite sweltering temperatures. He looked lost. Out of place. Like he could just keep walking forever. "You'd better go get him," she turned to me with a smirk.

I didn't want to, because he had never called, and the weeks since he had left had been a purgatory of waiting by the phone, ordering drinks at the Fairy Bar to pass the time, hoping he would appear in the jungle of fake flowers and plastic fairy wings. But something inside me was sparked when I saw his retreating form on the beach that day. I knew I would never see him again if I let him get away.

I sprinted down the beach calling his name. He only heard me when I was almost upon him and turned to greet me with what I would later identify as a guilty look. At the time I took it as innocent surprise. I jumped into his arms and wrapped my legs around his bony hips, kissed him, and asked him where he had been as if we were really lovers; as if we were in love.

He played along, saying that the search for work took longer than he expected. "It didn't pan out to much," he said. "Like most things."

His weak arms couldn't hold me and he soon put me down and dug through his jacket for his bottle of whiskey. I realized then why he always wore his heavy leather cloak, even in the scorching heat of the Mediterranean summertime—it was a giant holster for his booze. He took a long swig off the bottle and offered me one. I, of course, accepted.

"Did you read *The Master and Margarita*?" I asked, eyes shining at the man I thought I had retrieved from a state of disappearance, from becoming just a memory.

Harry's lips arched into his graceful version of a guilty smile and pulled the book out of his pocket. It was shriveled, browned, and crusty.

"I got in a fight with a Moroccan. He stabbed me in the hand and the book got covered in blood, so I couldn't read it?" With the accent, everything was a question. Or maybe it was just Harry.

"Oh," I said. I envisioned the fight in my mind, an elegant battle on the streets of Madrid, a scene much better than any book I'd ever read. The story of his battle literally bled through the pages; rendering the words useless and inscrutable. The book was part of Harry's adventure now. Just a prop in the Odyssey of his life, which seemed to be a

series of strangely glamorous situations over which he had no control. I nodded…I understood. Did he?

We agreed to meet later that night at the Fairy Bar, which in Harry's absence I had realized was a good metaphor for our relationship. A fantasy. You could never tell if Harry did things like that on purpose; whether there was any thought at all going into his actions, even though they often felt heavy with meaning. If he did, he hardly knew it himself. Like his subconscious was painting a picture that he wasn't aware of.

I asked him if he had slept with his ex-girlfriend. He said he hadn't. "She wouldn't do it?" he said. Whiskey glistened like diamonds on his lips. I thought his honesty was endearing. At least he admitted he had tried.

We continued to see each other for several months following. I convinced him to play slow contemplative games of chess in the Gaudi Park, expecting to witness a hidden talent that would reveal his true inner intelligence. But if he won it was by accident, clumsily moving his queen to reveal an elaborately clever checkmate proving that I was, in fact, pinned far beyond escape. An elegant plan that he never intended to put into motion. Most of the time I won, and he didn't try.

One day he showed up carrying Salman Rushdie's *Satanic Versus* and I asked him what it was about. "I'm not quite sure, to tell you the truth. I just picked it up to kill time."

It got to the point where he couldn't get out of bed without a tall glass of whiskey to propel him into the day. It consumed him. I considered him to be a form of genius; the kind that can't face the world without a drink because the world is too painful. Being sober was like going skiing without sunglasses on—it just burns the eyes. He disappeared more and more, and when he was gone, all I could do was wait for him to reappear, like a ghost, because I had no way of contacting him and he never called. I didn't even know where he lived.

In the middle of January, I was going to the South of Spain for a few weeks and tried to find him to tell him my plans. As if he were a lover who would care; as if, maybe, he would come. I thought a trip to the south might peak his interest; just out of curiosity he might fall into the car and we'd drive away together as a happy couple, like trapping an animal with a piece of apple and peanut butter. But I never found him and I left, sadly unable to report to anyone at all my plans.

By the time I returned to Barcelona, I had accepted the fact that he had disappeared. Until one morning, after coffee, I took a walk down to the bridge by my apartment that stretched over a large dusty ravine. Harry was stumbling home over the bridge, and I could tell by the way he was walking that he was just returning after a long night out. He saw me, swung his head lazily and squinted his sapphire eyes at me through the glare of the Spanish sun. We met eyes and he turned away, brushing his wild hair back like he always did when he was nervous. This time he didn't bother to explain.

PHYLLIS FRANK

DISORDER

I'm going to start at the end this time—
I just killed a spider that was crawling on my wall.
Tonight all of the carpets, three area rugs
and three sofas in my house are clean,
very, very clean, steam cleaned, in fact.
The getting dried out and back to normal
takes longer than you think.
The carpet is still damp under my feet.
This morning, I was still picking up belongings,
putting them on top of the beds, or in the bathrooms,
or on spare patches of laminate flooring.

I wanted to make it easy for the carpet cleaners.
I wanted them to notice that I was organized,
that I had it all under control, that I was prepared.
I am always wanting people to think I'm organized.
I am always trying to distract from the disorder
and the disarray of my real true life.
The fingerprints on the stainless-steel appliances,
the cobwebs where the walls meet at right angles,
the dirty laundry dumped by the kitchen door,
the aftershocks from the death of a parent.
I am indebted to the carpet cleaners.
That I have made my spaces more serene—
gone is the clutter that can telegraph the beats of a life—
the bills, the explanation of insurance benefits,
the absentee ballots, the junk mail,
the condolence cards.

But I am deceptive, and I am superficial.
I have taken shortcuts and I am disorderly.
My closet floors have never been steam-cleaned.
Clothes and suitcases and papers and storage boxes
and sheets and towels and blankets
and Swiffer pads and shoes
and empty shoe boxes and photographs
and a broken sex toy and an old baby blanket
and my last wedding dress
are stuffed into and piled high in my closet.
My sister is getting sucked under tsunami
waves of grief from losing our mother.
She is the one who had to throw out the deflated balloons
and the dead yellow tulips from the celebration of life.
I am the one who found time to learn

how to play Mah-Jongg.
All of the stains on my carpet are gone now,
except for the hot pink Gatorade ones that my ex-husband
left behind in the guest bedroom.
The carpet cleaner told me again those
stains will never come out.
I've told my sister that she can still communicate
with our mother, just in a different way.
She's said that it's not working,
so, I crack my knuckles
and make a plan to rip up the stained carpet.

LUMPS

The squishy compression of the pale flesh
The eyes of tumbling LEGO blocks
Possessor of a depressive resume
Almost hairless, a luscious cantaloupe
Next to fossilized scarabs in the landing gear
Maraschino cherry nipples, buds-o-mine
Toothless at one orifice and chartreuse at the other
Don't wait for the blood-stained pantyhose in Act II
Wailing, dimpled, delicious baby-faced slut
Awake now with fingers in mouth
To suck, to burp, to dream, to shit, to live

A blazing waterfall of cascading rocks
Hydration and innate self-lubrication
One antelope-eaten sweater vest piled low
Rosy, nubbin, dark red tulip vessel
Learn by doing, take risk plunging into
A clitoral street fight, journey of a pauper
Dream catcher Zuni warrior blinks
Thigh high leather boots broadcast
Prepubescent breasts in mist
Pubic spaces lie fallow
Languid copper re-piping, a specialty
Scandinavian reservations unending
Tongue moistened lips open wide
Sweet snake to the mystical spot
Please provide servicing on the Westside
Ready the perfect binding for my publisher

LIKE A DAY IN MAY

Oxygen saturation putrefying now
Festering wounds that refuse to salute
Scotch-taped and paper clipped gyrations
Beguiling fuck off in the ninth inning
Consolation elusive and desiccated
Doggy style indiscretion, a technicality
Amorous, taut, feverish, gliding
Gravity precludes anxious penetration
The chanteuse is a singing badass
Get the shit out into the john
St. Christopher protect the hearts and hands

Decadence ferments the best of us
Rigid mucous membranes slouch at the ready
Call me Lolita in the tormented everglades
Cease and desist with that totem pole
Adios to the metaphysical tango
Alias Smith & Wesson tendrils try to climb the fence
Changes in cardiac syncopation duly noted
Spawning salmon pause and cry tears of bile
So glad we could come again and again and again
The thank you notes are in the mail
Yielding to the corroded stop signs
I whisper to the saccharine damp earth
Listen for once you son-of-a-bitch
I've got something to say

SHANDY GABBAY

THE MOUTH OF LIFE

Lured by untamed desire
a primal need to feel
the breath of existence, I crave
to kiss the mouth of life.

Devil-red lips drenched
in wine, dripping
with seductive deceit,
devour me raw
with reckless abandon.
Temptation quivers
through my veins, emptying
into the arterial reservoir of my churned heart.

Wanton thoughts float
in lucid circles, expelling
all that is real and sensible,
my suffocating spirit yearning to be resuscitated,
my hollow heart beating with echo and excitement,
my heavy chest heaving, leaving me
without breath. Somewhere between
life's enchanted forest of disillusion
and the convoluted delusions
of my schizophrenic head
sits a deep-rooted, Darwinian desire
to need, to want, to feel.

Tease me, tantalize me,
take me by the tongue, take me
to the secret garden, whisper
sweet nothings of a utopian fortitude filled
with perfume-laced cherry blossom paths of pleasure.
Make me wet with fertile soil,
turn green my withered leaves
dress my branchless soul

with primrose buds bursting unbridled ambition.

Swallow me whole
with hunger and heed, save me
from the anesthetized nothing I've become, save me
from the wicked self of a superficial world, save me
from this fearless cataclysmic macrocosm of predators.

Lightning crashes
pent-up tears release
in jealous storms of rage, pouring
into tide pools of betrayal.
Fluttering leaves surrender
to winter's burly blast, tempest winds of wrath
twirl into a vortex of outrage and hate
gusts of uncontrolled passion blast like bullets
blazing through my heart, turning breath to death,
the kiss, an inferno burning through me—
burning, burning,
burning me alive.

Disenchanted fantasies pulverize to ashes,
desperate thoughts consume my trembling heart
the cynical reality of a makeshift world
painted with brushstrokes of charred rainbow colors
baseless thoughts now broken dreams,
sought after whims now worthless possessions,
stolen kisses now my stolen heart, a flattened heart
contorted and detached,
tattered and torn, botched and butchered
beaten down, damaged and defective.
Lost somewhere
in the scorched drought-stricken trenches
of that evil garden.
I am broken, soul stripped down and buried
beneath the flat earth I once thought round.

Love, you lying bastard, beast,
you cold-blooded crooked creep,
you preaching breaching illusion of eternal bliss
faking, fooling, feeling me up
then letting me down and leaving me
naked and afraid to rot and rest
out of strength to break
free from the self-destructive, self-inflicted
self-flagellating discontent
of a strait-laced life.

Love, you seething, deceiving,
misleading seductress
hiding under the devil's breath
sitting oh-so-discreet on the tip of life's tongue
once the sweet lullaby of kindred souls
now the rancid aftertaste

of chastised dreams, forever etched
in time. Love remains
a dance in isolation,
a solo moonlight sonata
played and replayed
played and replayed
played and replayed
penetrated by this nothingness, fucked
by the circle of life.

ALICIA GAREY

THE BIRD

It was in the garden of my apartment building
gray and motionless, on its side, permanently asleep.
As small as my young hand,
not including the little stick legs
so fragile like twigs.

It was fall,
brown trees and pale sky.
I was seven or eight and close to the ground.
It was quiet and I was alone, like many other days.
My first sighting of a dead thing, aside from bugs.
Poor bird, I thought. Exposed with no one to honor it.
I knew I had to bury it. Afraid to touch it,
I found a piece of dirty cardboard, covered the little
creature and layered it with dried leaves
But first, I stared for a while.
One tiny jewel eye open.
I could almost hear how it had once chirped.

I remember my shock, the truth of a little death.
I thought of the bird every so often. Never told anyone—
I didn't say I had buried a bird that day.
It was our time together,
I had been assigned to do it.

It's possible the bird was cleaned away
or the east coast winds blew it out of its protective cover
of paper and leaf, or an animal ate it
in the middle of the night. I knew even its death
was temporary until it would evaporate
or become part of the earth.

Maybe one day I'd think about the bird again
and write a story from so long ago
before the rest of my own life began.

REBEKAH HOWLAND

CUT SHORT

let's get real now
for our time is suddenly
cut short
let's say exactly what we mean
oh, you always did
that's right
it was me
who held back
self-consciously
in fear and inhibition
now we stand
together
a match like no other
and there it is
no more time to lose

CHESTER AND ZARAFA

"Sorry," said Zarafa, the tall elegant giraffe, standing near an acacia tree in her spacious pen. Her long purple tongue was intertwined in the high tender leaves she was munching. She had bumped Chester's foot by accident just seconds before, through the fence.

"I don't like the way things are," said Chester, the young black coarse-haired chimp. Although his pen was favorably located next to Zarafa's, it felt too small for him, and too remote from his other friends.

"But that's the way things are," insisted Zarafa. The layout of the zoo was convoluted. It was inconveniently arranged for the handful of animals living there who were devoted friends, and liked to socialize in person at dusk, just after the zoo closed.

"Hey, would you look at that?" asked Chester. Resting up against Zarafa's wooden stable was an enormous abstract painting, glittering in the afternoon sun light. Barely distinguishable were the abstract shapes of a lion, a giraffe, and two chimps, suggestive of a mother and child.

"I've never seen anything like it" exclaimed Zarafa. The painting was mesmerizing in its beauty and adorned by an ornate frame flecked with flakes of real gold leaf. Staring at it might send one into a trance or perhaps even into a state of ecstasy.

"It reminds me of something though," said Chester thoughtfully. Chester looked so young and innocent having just been trimmed and immaculately groomed. He wore a metal tag around his left foot embedded with tiny diamonds which read "Chester." Chester had been rescued at a very young age from the house of a famous abstract artist and

had been exposed to magnificent pieces of modern art. The artist however had suddenly deserted both their home and Chester.

Do you remember the house at the end of Cedar Street? asked Zarafa tenderly. Zarafa had an excellent memory. She had accompanied the zookeeper on the mission that day when Chester had been a baby, to the house at the end of Cedar Street—the day they rescued Chester. She could not believe how tiny and helpless Chester had looked that day hiding in an upstairs bedroom of the decadently appointed house.

Yeah, said Chester. The look on his face was very sad and his body posture spelled dejection. If he hadn't been a chimp, he probably would have cried. The oppressive heat hung over them and did not help Chester's mood. It was a dusty day. The water in Zarafa's water trough looked clean though, and hopefully it was cool enough to drink. At the base of her trough in the dirt laid a quarter-sized shiny red ruby.

Why? asked Zarafa. She wondered if Chester really remembered the house. It was two-storied, covered with red ivy and exotic vines in front, and the backyard looked like an overgrown orchard of ragged banana trees. There was plenty of fruit to eat and plenty of vines to swing on. But Zarafa had remembered something more than that there. It was just a trace. Some trace lingered of the mother Chester had once known.

No reason, replied Chester. He rarely thought of the old house and he could not remember his mother, other than perhaps a fading shadow on dark nights. He had convinced himself that he was happy enough living at the zoo where he was safe, close to Zarafa, and to a few of his other animal friends.

Maybe we'd better just both go home, Zarafa and Chester uttered in nearly perfect unison. They meant it was time to get bedded down for the night; Chester in a favorite tree, and Zarafa in her wooden stable, against which the abstract masterpiece still leaned, gleaming in the afternoon rays of the sun. Tomorrow would bring a new day and perhaps it would also bring some answers to the mysteries of this one.

SANDRA K

HE SAID HE WOULD KILL ME

On some level I am still terrified. Terrified of being noticed. Terrified of letting myself shine. Terrified of really being seen. I watch as the people around me LOVE to be seen. Not me. I want to sit in the back of the bus and have no one notice. Being seen means being hurt. Raped. Muffled to the point of losing consciousness. He certainly didn't want my mother, or my brothers, to hear my muffled cries.

I learned over the years to be quiet, to leave my body, to let him have his way. What was the use in fighting when I was 40 pounds and he was 200? Surviving meant giving in.

But I didn't want to live. I tried to kill myself in all sorts of ways that seemed clever to a small child. When I was five I watched Craig, my best friend who I knew I was going to marry, accidentally run through a closed sliding glass door. He had a chunk missing from his head, and blood pouring out of the hole. Everyone thought he was going to die. "Is he ok?" I squeaked out. Time stood still. His normally gregarious mom was holding a wet bloody dishtowel to his head and crying. There were shards of glass all over the playroom floor, the grey carpet glistening like stars as the bright summer sun reflected off the mess. We kids stared at our friend who was bleeding out and in a state of shock, his striped t-shirt now wet with red. "Call an ambulance!" the mom shouted to her husband.

Craig survived, but this gave me ideas. I decided to try falling down the open staircase in my parents' mid-century house. Along the back of the staircase was a two story window, and my goal was to go through it. But being five, I hadn't accounted for the size of my small body and the gap between the window and the platform on the stairs. When I fell, I hit the window and slipped into that gap, dangling by my head which didn't fit through.

Another time I peddled like mad on my little banana bike down a steep hill. I slammed head-on into a roadblock halfway down the hill, and was thrown over the bike and over the roadblock into a nasty thicket of thorny bushes. Again, not my best idea. I ended up scratched and bruised and grounded from using my bike. But still alive.

I wanted nothing more than to beat him to it. I wanted out. He said he would kill me if I told anyone, so it was never going to stop unless I took my life. Or he did. As I grew up I didn't care about sustaining life, or my body.

As a teenager, I would drink until I'd black-out and pass out. It didn't take much—I've never had much of a tolerance for alcohol. Luckily, I had good friends who would watch over me, make sure I was okay and made it home.

When I was in my 20s, having just moved to San Francisco, I bought a scooter to get around town on and never wore a helmet. I loved riding around with the wind in my hair, darting between cars and carelessly splitting lanes. I told my mother that if I died on my scooter she should take solace in knowing that I had died happy. I didn't care if my life ended. I never expected to live this long, or to even make it to 30.

ROSLYN KIRSHMAN

TO MY SAMMY
–in eternal love

A broken bamboo stalk
muted
I stand steeped
in the silent sands
of my heart's
wasteland
no more hollow
or passionate illusions
I was me
because you were you
my undaunted Homeric hero
and soul-mate
now the me that is left
weeps alone
screaming in anger
into an inferno
of private pain
and primal shame
bereft of breath
trapped in an eternal
tomb of tears.

ALLISON KOEHLER

THE STAINED EDGES OF PRUSSIAN BLUE
The soft edges of Prussian blue
stained fireworks
thrown beside
a collection of compliments
folded into silk
like nipples the size of buttons
and skin
soft as oiled contours
say what is true
it is the senses
but maybe if we touch
mystery will be outlined in lead
the ruby is
inspiration is
erotic
best exploded
into the nighttime constellation
of whispers

ALL I CAN SEE IS THE WHITE SILICONE
All I can see is the white silicone

gluing together everything unanticipated
covered wood painted poivre
straight lines you would never give
without demand
scraping the lead sides
while nettles soften in butter
and you pretend you are wearing
only an apron
guarded from every grandmother
behind tinted sand
you foresaw nothing past the flowers
because you aren't a maker of doors
lazy about craft or responsibility
but you aren't a child either
simply because tenderness
makes us strip and scream
what can be made
material is so much nothing
molten tin will
how much do you trust your self doubt
no truth to not reach for
and perceived disappointment is
always your own
so give us the ones with more space between each rainbow
you know what to ask
you know what is a farm ghost imagined
and what is, and what can be

REGITZE LADEKARL

THE SCROLLING PANDA
A panda was scrolling through its Instagram feed when it saw an ad for adult toys. It thought I am almost six years old, and I am often bored in this zoo; I should get me one of those. So, it ordered the toy online, and a few days later it arrived because of fast shipping. The panda was mighty pleased. It unpacked the toy and threw the box and the bubble wrap in the blue bin for recycling. It read through the inserted quick start instruction sheet three times and felt confident in how to operate it.

The panda loved its toy. It played with it every day and sometimes two or three times. In the beginning, it would only use it in the little cave at the back of the enclosure because pandas can be shy. But then the nannies visiting the zoo complained to the zoo experience manager as they had promised the kids in their care that they would get to see a panda and if they did not, the kids' parents would turn the nannies into ICE and have them deported.

The zoo experience manager told this to the head of zookeeping, who then mistakenly called a meeting with the single-colored bear manager. He wanted to give her an earful because this was the seventh time the bears had been caught hibernating on the job, and the head of zoo keeping had been looking for a reason to fire her so he could give the job to his son-in-law whose name was Jared as the convention goes. The single-colored bear manager countered with suing the zoo for genus discrimination which was settled out of court for a partially undisclosed two-digit amount.

With time, the panda did get word that the public had to see more of it. It thought, that is not a problem; I'll bring my toy with me. And so, it did. Now the panda enjoyed its toy where everyone could see it. Some children laughed, many cried, and even more asked questions. A teacher was fired because she posted pictures of the third-grade field trip on the school website. She might have had a solid legal case but opted to retrain as an e-sport gymnast instead and went on to become very successful.

The zookeeper who was assigned to the panda exhibit had less luck. When he tried to take the toy away from the panda, it used on the zookeeper instead. To this day he is not able to stand up straight or contract his sphincter, and he never won anything on his scratch tickets. That goes to prove that it is rarely a good idea to stop a bear from masturbating in public.

NOREEN LAWLOR

TEMPTRESS

I became a golden weasel, small and sleek
beguiling in a pale blond way. My body slipped
around and under fences, sometimes slithering

like a snake, sometimes with catlike grace
flattening itself with an almost purr. So sensual
and lithe had my body become that I glided

always in an amber haze. My fur was luxurious
as angora and exuded the musky aroma of myrrh.
In short, I was exquisite and irresistible. I mesmerized

my prey with topaz eyes until my tiny sharp white teeth
bit sensuously into their longing necks. I knew the
ecstatic thrill, their breath merging with my own

their moment of amethyst mingling with my coral blood.

Humans loved, venerated me as a demigod
tried to trap me in their temples, lure me
with choicest morsels of muskrat and hare.

Sometimes, on moonlit ridges they encountered me
or under a snowbank with great Orion rising overhead.
Once I let a beautiful young hunter stroke my fur

giving him only the swiftest of bites to remember me by.
I moved through woods and desert terrain, alternately
leaping and rubbing my soft belly
into the earth's dark burrows.

STELLASUE LEE

FLAT

on my back, I look up to identify
shapes that appear out of a concrete ceiling—

a small child holds out her hands,
a puppy with black eyes and a slight

imperfection for its nose. There are
many others to keep me company

as light plays from the cars six stories
below—an old woman, her mouth

round with surprise, a boat,
afloat in ripples made by the pour.

Once, when I was feverish, I saw the
most amazing thing. It was early morning,

I think, and the ceiling became liquid—
waves lapping at walls, but later,

the concrete seemed to have set again
and I didn't worry enough to sort it out.

That night there were church bells.
I slept in uneven shadows, woke hungry.

FRONT PORCH SITTING

It has been a brutal summer.
I could almost forget except for
the testimony of parched plants and bushes
scorched by sun.
Even now the sun hides behind tall trees,
backlighting those by the creek path.
There is a coyote den there. Pups announce
their presence during full-moon nights.

My mother walks up the front steps and sits heavily
in an opposing chair as night closes in.
The dead seem to have little to say, so we don't say
much of anything

for not knowing where to start. When everything
is encompassed by the pitch black, I return inside

and leave her sitting there. Morning bears witness
to each crushed cushion.

BEVERLY MAGID

MOTHER'S DAY, 2019
When it's Mother's Day I think about her,
gone for so many years,
I try to dwell on her large luminous eyes,
grey with green flecks,
rounded cheeks, like those of a young schoolgirl,
flushed with the discovery of life.
Let's forget the pain, the moods changing
as swiftly as a summer storm,
no more flashing anger or questions
of Why, Why, Why?
There was once laughter and a soft bosom to cling to—
surprises on birthdays, kisses goodnight,
but always lurking, just in the shadows, a tear, a sigh,
but for whom?
Me, my father, or that baby
who never breathed a second breath,
who left us without a name, but stayed with us forever.

FATHER'S DAY, 2019
He died as he lived, quietly but strong, no complaints
Just a plaintive "Is that me,"
when he saw himself in the mirror—
body shrunk, eyes sunken, hands unsteady.
Where was the strong man
who carried me on his shoulders,
who taught me that a promise is to be kept,
no matter what, that honesty was not only the best policy,
but the only way to live?
He still shone inside that wasted body,
fighting until the last breath,
teaching me that life is a treasure to be cared for,
a jewel to be worn proudly.
I carry his humor, cradle his words, whisper his name—
Father, rest easy.

SHARA MCCALLUM

MEMORY
I bruise the way the most secreted,
most tender part of a thigh exposed
purples then blues. No spit-shine shoes,
I'm dirt you can't wash from your feet.
Wherever you go, know I'm the wind
accosting the trees, the howling night
of your sea. Try to leave me, I'll pin you

between a rock and a hard place; will hunt you,
even as you erase your tracks
with the tail ends of your skirt. You think
I'm gristle, begging to be chewed?
No, my love: I'm bone. Rather: the sound
bone makes when it snaps. That ditty
lingering in you, like ruin.

SHE
She could sing the blue out of water
She could sing the meat off a bone
She could sing the fire out of burning
She could sing a body out of home

She could sing the eye out of a hurricane
She could sing the fox right out its hole
She could sing the devil from the details
She could sing the lonely from a soul

She could sing a lesson in a yardstick
She could sing the duppy out of night
She could sing the shoeless out of homesick
She could sing a wrong out of a right

She could sing the prickle from the nettle
She could sing the sorrow out of stone
She could sing the tender from the bitter
She could sing the never out of gone

GRIEF
I linger, rearranging the furniture,
making the sky contract
till it no longer contains the horizon.
When I hover, you hear cicadas crescendo.
You mistake me for winter's onset
or the body as it ages. Foolish girl.
You console yourself with fables
where straw is spun to gold
yet a promise remains unpaid.
Have you really not yet learned?
Only in fairy tales is disaster averted
with a secret word. In this world,
magic claims no dominion.
Death is a door, which keeps opening.

CATFISH MCDARIS

TATTOOED LOVE
My old man played the blues
and dragged me from Biloxi,
to Chicago, and Paris, one day he
quit speaking and forgot his guitar.

He sat in a chair for five years
eating chicken and drinking whiskey,
then he turned into a butterfly before
my eyes and flew out the window.

I woke with a dog shit tongue, my
chest was covered with a dried
blood soaked towel, it was saffron
colored and stank of tequila.

A tattoo of Jesus walking on water
adorned my freshly shaved torso.
holy guacamole I thought, now I'll
probably be touched by the finger of God.

I met a beautiful Mexican senorita,
she said, "You're tired and I am too.
But we are two different animals,
you need rest, I am run over,

worn bald at the edges and can't
get much traction. With time you
will rejuvenate. I am a black chunk
of rubber on the road of life."

We traveled north to the valley of chilis
hanging crimson from adobe vigas, at
night we slept under a Frida Kahlo moon
dancing horses licked our faces awake.

BEATNIK BLUES
The night moaning like a whore faking
love, red neon pouring whiskey on junk-
ies watching their blood ejaculate up into
a syringe, eyelids fluttering on Whitman's
finger, dance boys dance, blow your har-
monica until sunshine orange drenches
the shadows, prisons, and asylums over
flow, spewing detritus, talking rats with
yellow jaundiced eyes and bebop cats

William S. Burroughs cut off his finger
in 1939 out of love for Jack Anderson
and sent it to Arnold Gingrich at *Esquire*,
later he said it was an initiation for the
Crow Indian tribe, he hoped his words
would be published, Gingrich sent Bur-
roughs a note back reading, "I greet you
at the beginnings of a wonderful career,
when do I get the corpse?" William had
love for heroin, morphine, and marijuana

His work was of mystical, occult, and mag-

ical themes, William's totem animal was a
green reindeer, his life was fleeing from one
troubled place to another, he killed his second
wife, Joan in 1951 while drunk and went to
prison in Mexico City for 13 days, they had
him for culpable homicide, he fled to Morocco
where he was accused of importing opiates, he
fled to a rundown hotel in the Latin Quarter of
Paris, to meet Ginsberg, Corso, and Orlovsky.

Burroughs cooked the dragon with a burnt spoon,
a step ahead of the law, snapping fingers, to the
bongo beat, chasing daydreams down the street.

THE MAN THAT BROUGHT A SINGING FAT LADY AND A VIOLIN TO A GUNFIGHT
Of all that is written I only love what is written in blood.
—Nietzsche

Surrounded by dead guardian angels
listening to: The Mephistopheles of
Los Angeles by Marilyn Manson

Warming hands and face above a hell
fire in a 55-gallon barrel dreaming of
dancing with a senorita in Guadalajara

Palm trees figs and dates in Damascus
driving Thunderbirds through a sequoia
and zebras and swallowtails in the Mojave

Shackled by my years, gravity sucking
my energy, the sky, and ceilings piss
on my head, the walls yawn in boredom,

Nobody laughs at the ugly mirror, guns
mean noise and chaos, death should be up
close and personal with a lovely serenade.

CHEROKEE ROSE
Prolonging the heartbreak, baby
baby, your love leaves me on a
ten story ledge watching the side
walk artists below creating master-

Pieces vanishing in the rain, they
smile like hundred-dollar bills are
pouring down, they know that every
thing is temporary even blossoms

Floating on the xeric wind, apricots
and nectarines make fiery love and
replace the sun in the cinnamon sky,
watching a video of Tommy Castro

And the Painkillers, play his song,
Ride, pretty ladies dancing, while he
Kerouac struts past City Lights Books,
keeping me alive like a Cherokee Rose.

ZOE MESSENGER

THE TOOL

I have a lot of clothes. My dad always says, "stop buying ripped jeans, I'll martini them for you!"

When I was in NY my dad and I went to Minetta Tavern, my favorite "fancy, old-timey steakhouse" in the city besides Leprechaun Luger. When the host saw us, she gave us the best table in the house. She thought he was my 'daddy' not my dad. He's a good-looking guy and when I put on makeup and dress up…well…I still look like a kid, but *Vanity Fair* fell for it!

Our table was a romantic corner booth that looked out over the whole restaurant, the scene. But the table was shaking, it was uneven. We told them we needed to fix it before our wedding-de-bouffe for two came with bone marrow etcetera. The waiter said, "No problem I'll get the tool." Two minutes later a perfectly cut, smoldering tall Michelangelo in uniform started walking towards us. My dad said, "Hey? I think that's our tool!"

MAGGIE MORRIS

PSYCHOPATHIC NARCISSISTIC LOVE ADDICT

Whip smart surfboard sneaker fix Listerine drunk car scribble peacock phony pie cheese board toy stuffed sea ranch lovesick diamond fox thick choke sushi love.

Congratulations.

Bullet dick blast chop school fake line journal snoop fentanyl farm plot cover-up two-faced garden hose baby leg let go wonderland woo woo shove it power tripper snivel drip why you wanna to fight foil dog shits on your kid's rug and you call her a psycho can't talk now marker stain nip nose book test street squash fish eye bag vented drama addict with a weed farm.

Black hole paleo funk beat prophylactic half shirt push wipe gyno prick draw blood tear face foolish siren lies motherfucker lies broken doll can't help alibi prenup two lines dotted lines on the line another line.

Good girl nice girl sweet girl 911 girl your girl another girl remembers when I found your cancer and snipped the stitches out itchy whisper freckle fantasy.

Complaint department concealer won't hide victim child nope smudge in the ass precious first then tranny bump ex-squad Sandy Allie Lizzie Sarah Lindsay Leslie Denise on the altar but for private jet Helen fuck Wyatt Venus Irish tit pics in Canada and now Karen poor Karen.

Google history.

Erase.

JEFF NEWMAN

SEASON CLOSED

I was sitting in the middle of my living room in my Dad's favorite armchair, the green tartan one, the one with the right arm shredded by our cat Max, the one with his left eye missing. I was sitting inside my favorite sweatshirt, the one with the dual images of the birds and the fishes, the one with the dual images of the birds and the fishes devouring each other. I was sitting in the middle of an otherwise boring Saturday afternoon, the one like every other boring Saturday afternoon, the one like every other boring Saturday afternoon had been since we moved to here. I was sitting and watching and sitting. I was sitting and watching and sitting and watching them. I was sitting and watching and sitting and watching them go at it.

"Great," he said, "just fucking great. Here we are, another week's gone, and nothings on the books."

"I can't stand the thought," she said, "of sacrificing another one just for the privilege of His Nibs' smile."

"Well," he said, "what are we gonna tell the Big Man when he finally shows up? How're you gonna explain away this mess?"

"Don't we have enough to do," she said, "what with finding clean water every day before the curfew?"

"When are you gonna relax," he said, "and just do the one thing that I've ever asked you to do? Why does it have to be so hard?"

"Damn it," she said, "you know I can't focus, not with that fucking soap opera playing in the background."

"You know the fires are real," he said, "right?"

"Yeah," she said, "yeah, I do."

I was sitting and watching and sitting and watching in the middle of my living room in my dad's favorite armchair. I was feeling the dread deep. I was praying for the coming of the avenging angel.

RHODA NOVAK

THE AUCTION

I cringe and shudder.
Auctioned off to the highest bidder.

Men gather next to me—chomping cigars.
I am naked—shrouded in smoke and fog.
Opening my mouth, "Great set of teeth."

Men poke. "Don't disturb the merchandise."
Men withdraw tobacco stained hands.
"What great hips. She'll bear many children."

I blanch and shiver uncontrollably.
"Nice firm butt. Do I hear $100?"
I say, "But I'm a physicist."
He drops his gavel and sets me free.

HURRICANE CLEO

Pulling my raincoat tight,
I struggle into my car
And enter the causeway.

I miss an oncoming car.
Swerve to stay on the road.

Angry waves lap at my tires.
Sheets of rain blind me.
Cars skidding.
Lightning flashes.
Destruction illuminated.

My heart flutters.
My hands shake.
One mistake.
My last.

Howling dogs.
Inky black sky.
Thunder crackles.
Glass shatters.
Transformers explode.

Clammy sweat.
Salty mouth.

Palm frond bounces off hood.
Barely misses windshield.

Fear I'd pushed down
Rises like a tsunami

Engulfs me.
Is this how want to I die?

DOROTHY PINCUS

I LOVE ME SOME GRAPES

I'm sitting here waiting, waiting for my pen to start writing. But nothing happened, Wow, is this what they call writers block?

So, I sit and wait. The Jeopardy theme song is playing in my head.

The pressure is on now to create something magical. You see, I pushed against my fears of writing and finally joined a writing class to be judged, ignored, or be a part of something more than me, myself and I.

I love being alone, but not lonely. It a strength of mine, it just feels normal to me. Most of my life, I've shared my thoughts and feelings through journaling. The fact is, now that I have an assignment to journal, which is something I'd done since I was a kid, my journal writing is jealous or upset that I might be changing our connections, Journal says, I'm cheating. Hahahahaha, you can't cheat on journal writing right?

Yes, you can Dorothy, I have been your go-to your whole entire life and now you wanna trade me for Grapes?

What does Grapes have that I don't give you, I gave you my soul, my life, my solutions to your messed up complicated world and now, you want to give me a Facebook status, it's complicated.

My response to journal, Dear Journal, thank you so much for sticking with me my whole life. You have gotten me out of some difficult moments and for that I'm internally grateful. I would never trade you in or substitute you. You and I are one of the same. You are my water, I can't live without you.

Grapes, I enjoy Grapes. Grapes are sweet, chewy, and healthy. Grapes adds a different dimension of writing experience. A different taste to try my palate. I also, love the color of grapes too. Some grapes are green, yellow, deep dark purple and I especially love the seedless grapes. The cotton grapes are too sweet, but that's just me.

So, you see Journal, you have nothing to worry about. You still hold my deepest innermost darkest and bravest secrets.

I know you feel neglected right now, but in time you will see, I'm am not taking away anything, but we are only gaining a family member. This is our new normal, think of Grapes at step-father or a long-lost relative we have been looking for and we called on Dr. Phil to help us find them. We have to mature in order to grow so we won't be stuck on a one-dimension level. I think it's time to be a part of a team, so we can be taught by a gifted guru, grand master of Grapes. Let's think outside of the box but most importantly learn technique to enhance our beautiful life. Journal, I love you and I will agree to always love you.

JULIE RICO

THE RATS WORE STARCHED WHITE SHIRTS

I work hard. Hard work is all I know. I was poor. I am afraid of being poor. I find my self-worth is attached to my work. Without work what am I worth? I am not a worthy person. I was laid off from the Truck plant and became a shell of a person. The value of me was in my blue-collar job. I was nothing without that job. I am nothing.

The cavern of grey cement buzzing clanging moving now muted made impotent, useless to me now. A trickle became a river down their faces. The tsunami of men so great, crushed to pebbles on a forgotten beach. The rats wore starched white shirts to usher in a new world order. I found a vacant shell in my home.

I am a blue-collar worker. Blue-collar workers can't afford regret, that's for pussies. Work yourself into the ground is what we get. The rich people what do they get? They get carpe diem, joie de vivre—not us. We get the grind.

I was happy in the factory. I met my now- ex-husband. I made good money, I had vacation time. I was in a union. Where else can you get a job with those kinds of perks? After I was laid off, college was my only option. I am not sorry for going to college. But my life has never been as normal as it was when I worked in the factory.

Our home near the factory was filled with the smell of apple pies and elephants. Our factory smelled of crazy friends beyond the Milky Way. A grassy knoll in the front yard beckoned visitors—please rest. Kittens brought cinnamon candy love. Cinnamon candy embedded our minds with thoughts of the grassy knoll.

Empty shells walk sidewalks lost in a world with no maps.
Solid lives now effusive smiles beg to see your map.
The greed-soaked streets filled with potholes, no one will fix. Ethereal kindness now gone, the fires of hell beckon, come hither my child, there is so much more to see.
Keep on keepin' on is my new mantra. It's either that or I off myself which is really not an option at this young age. Anyway, there are too many fights left in me. My mom used to call me the little lawyer. My forte was arguing with whoever. I was good at it. I did not seek out arguments, I just ran into a lot of people with bad opinions.

I am dead now. The pit was dug deep. The rats did not want me back. They were happier taking all the money for themselves. They wanted an end to regulations. They wanted an end to providing a living wage. They wanted an end to equality for all. They wanted an end to feminism. They wanted an end to clean water. They wanted an end to clean air. They wanted an end to unions. They wanted an end to me. They wanted power, but most of all they wanted money.

LEDA ROGERS

THE SNAKE OF DEATH

My depression seems to be looming around the corner waiting with bated breath to catch me off guard. It has settled there in its warm place wanting me to say yes and give it life. I am tentative about reaching out to touch its comforting hand. If I do, it will grab hold of my hand, then my arm, my torso, my whole body and finally my mind. Not my mind! I cannot let it crawl through the synapses of achievement. My depression, the snake that it is, will wind its way into my soul and render it helpless. It will do its best to make me feel hopeless. It will rack my brain to change the way I think, and I will think only of death and destruction. I sit and think of distractions that will get me off the hook. Should I walk the dog? Maybe I should read. I'll try to write. Work on the computer, print out some photographs. I know, make some phone calls. To who? Wash the dishes. I don't want to do anything. I don't want to do anything. I don't want to do anything. I want to love somebody. I want to be in love. I want to be loved. I don't want to fall in love with my depression again. That is not the lover for me. It is only the enabler. Depression, you enable me to cry and feel sorry for myself, enable me to feel paralyzed, enable me to not care about myself, enable me to not care about anything, enable me to want to kill myself. I pull my hand away. You will not grab it this time. This time I control my thoughts. You cannot tug at my arm nor my torso, my body, nor my mind. You cannot wind your way into my soul this time. Not this time. My soul has made up its mind. I have decided to make my bed.

BARBARA ROTHSTEIN

THE VOICE OF THE TURTLE

They're all around us now,
the signs of permanent decline.
We said we loved the waters of our oceans,
our rivers, our lakes,
how they reflected the skies and the clouds,
the moonlight, the stars,
as if Monet had painted the liquid surfaces
of the earth around us.
But we never appreciated the bounty of these gifts,
or felt the reverence their beauty deserves.

We never thought to cherish and protect
the wonder of a violet,
the miracle of an oyster shell.
And still, we look away as the fish run out,
and as the last great century old turtle
struggles, collapsing in the thick murky sands,
her voice to be silenced forever.
Even as we feel the stinging rain falling from yellow skies
onto thick green waters, waters now choking for air,
waters we once saw as infinite, we close our eyes.
But the eyes of our Great Mother Earth are watching us.
They see us as the stiff-necked species we are.
The truth is, we hear the voice of the turtle
even as we proclaim our innocence.

MORE OR LESS

Less is more they say.
But the idea is more or less over my head.
When I had less, I worried more.
I was sure if I had more, I'd worry less.
Now that I have more, I have more to worry about.
I have more money, more stuff, more space,
more things than ever.
But I have less peace of mind.
It seems to me there are more e-mails and less purpose,
more comments less meaning,
more contacts less heart,
more likes less love.

GALI ROTSTEIN

RISE UP

I was emptying the dishwasher. I was empty. I was not full. I had no ideas. I had no ideas this morning. My mind was empty. I couldn't hear any thoughts. Last night from 2am to 4am I had a storm of thoughts. They came at me like one of those desert movies where the hero is at his desk under a white canopy tent dreaming. He lifts his eyes and sees a wall of roiling sand and clouds and lightning in the distance approaching fast. Before he can do anything more than dive under the desk and cover his head with a blanket, he is engulfed. In the dark, he can feel sand beneath him shifting. He can feel outlines of hard objects pushing against his bones. He is fortressed in a tomb of objects. The storm passes, the hero opens his eyes and sees the abundance of treasures uncovered by the blast of wind and sand over his excavation site. There is so much he cannot collect and catalogue at that moment and he is excited. He wants to stand up and shake off the sand, but he also wants to sleep. And now he is tired but cannot sleep. The gardeners have arrived. The whirl of the blower begins slicing through the quiet. I am standing at the sink in the kitchen. My mind is empty. I am tired. My head droops. My skull is covered in a-bed-of-grey tufts. It's a not so sexy version of bed head. My "do" is more like the Wooly Willy child's game that piles grey shavings on the cartoon metallic Willy head. It's post Chemo hair. I am tired, but I won the battle. The morning sun is hard at work shining down and drying up the puddles left by last night's rain. I can feel the crispness of the air in my mind. Under my apron I am wearing striped pajamas. It's a bad look for a Jewish girl, but I'm not Jewish, I am just Israeli. There is a razor blade on a leaf-shaped sponge. I use it to scrape shit that is hard to remove. We all live life on a razor's edge. The blower stops, allowing the bird's song to rise up.

LOOKING FOR MY DALI

I stand at the back door watching Eli sniff around. I have been thinking about death a lot lately. It's not the morbid death thoughts of a neurotic, with a pocket full of narcotics, just the actual circle of life acceptance. My father is 81 my dog is 11. Every few days I hear of a life ending. A friend loses her husband, another loses his mind. The garden hose is steadily dripping. The drops grow big before they fall one after the other. They are big and reflect the grey misty light of morning. The snails are out sliming across the Ice plants. There is one very brown one who is particularly slow. I imagine he is practicing for his personal mount Everest. He must have watched CNN last night. He must have seen how everyone climbs up that mountain at a snail's pace. Single file they ascend with Sherpas carrying households on their backs, just like his snail shell. He would carry his own shell. He would be slow and steady. He hears that at the peak people died waiting in line to descend. They couldn't wait. He can wait. He practices waiting all the time. Soft and snug inside his tiny house. Day for night, night for day. An infinite never-ending chain of electricity throughout the heavens and earth. The purple heart plant is sprinkled with dew. He will have a purple heart martini with three dew drops because some where it is 5 o'clock.

Every week people ask me how old is my good dog? He is truly a good dog, a great dog. If he was human he would be that guy that watches you from under his long black lashes, leaning up against a pillar, being the pillar, wearing black jeans that hug his boyish sexy ass, that supports his chiseled abdominal V, under a T-Rex concert T, inside a soft as butter well-worn vintage leather bomber. And he would only ever say a few words and each one would hold a universe, and strung together on silk thread, they would write a perfect song. A single black pearl found only in the belly of an oyster, in the depths of a womb like ocean. Liquid velvet cape. An opinion given so smoothly, that making a change would feel like a self-actualized option. "It works both ways, try each and see which resonates for you. It's all good. You are brilliant. Woof," he says.

I have been thinking about death a lot lately. I have been thinking about his death. I have been thinking about what I will ask him to do for us. For me. And he will. And I will. I will. I will go from dog to dog in search of my Dali. I will whisper, Eli? Beat. Do you remember the hole you chewed behind your chair? Beat. Eli? Beat. Do you like peanut butter? Beat. Eli? Is that your Sardine breath on my linen sofa? Wanna go to Mexico?

And a very small and soft and easily manageable, perfectly calm, born trained, with a heartbeat in sync with mine, newborn, will look up at me, beyond my eyes and say, "Woof, you are beautiful, I will rescue you. I love you so, so, so very much."

Eli barks hello to his squirrel friends from across the yard, then looks at me in case I will scold him because it's too early to make that much noise.

SUSAN SALOMON NEIMAN

MERMAID'S HAIR
I tell Alexa to play music I like
Don't know what she's playing
But I like it. Piano moving around the scales
But then Tony Bennet singing suicide is painless
No no, not that
No, this morning
Alexa off

This morning I noticed two things:
The blue ball is still in the stream but it's further down
Down trapped in the mermaid's hair
And my daughter who cannot decide
Whether to leave her husband
Left the top off the pen, I don't know why
But that drives me crazy
My husband does it too
No big deal, right? My husband is amazingly annoying
It's no big deal, right?
I like having him around

How much should I compromise?
I am not writing a novel or a memoir
Just anything that comes to mind
Anything I can find
That is the best I can do
Or is it? That's the critical voice
Second guessing
I've lived with her 75 years
That's my mother
A quarter of a century
So many bad times
Anorexia, bipolar, heroin addiction, depression,

Alienation, well at least were not poor

Back to my husband
I want the window open
He wants them shut
I open them after he goes to sleep
He watches sports
I watch period pieces
I want to go to Esalen
He wants to go to Las Vegas

He doesn't listen to my poetry

But he does the dishes
And laughs at my jokes when he can hear them
I am learning how to handle him
Know how to handle him
Take the good
Ignore the bad
No big deal? Right?

We play musical chairs at the dining table
I now sit next to him at the dining table
He is back in my heart
But my older daughter sits back at my table
Away from her unhappy marriage
My granddaughter is home from college
And she sits with her feet on the table
If I don't say something

I walk outside to look at the stream
The mermaid's hair has floated further downstream
And now resembles green islands in the black stream
The blue ball is no longer visible
A black crow stares at me from the tree branch
Caw caw cawing as if he owns the world
The frogs choir me
I am alone for a few moments
And I relish it

DEBRA SMALLEY

WHAT'S IN YOUR BASKET?
As I pushed my cart down the shelves of sodas, vinaigrettes and other bottled wets, at Ralphs on Sunset, I found the basket difficult to maneuver. So hard to push and nothing in it. Or is there? Can anyone see the heaviness I carry since forever? Being bullied, even into adulthood, was rough.

My grandfather, my papa, at 70 years old, was the first man who protected and defended me. He had my back and called out the man who spread lies about me. "Men who feel threatened, threaten," he said.

Last night, my papa came to me in a dream. He was dressed as I remembered in his brown silk vest under a wool camel-haired tan jacket. His gold watch fob, which I now treasure, hung from his black corduroy pant pocket. He hugged me and I felt total peace. "I miss you so much, I told him.

"I've missed you too," he said. Papa's charismatic comic book hero smile was so real. It was as if his passing 10 years ago at 90, never happened. Even so, nothing I found on the supermarket shelves could feed the hunger of my mirage. I suppress, I obsess, and I am depressed.

"Hi, Miss. Did you find what you're looking for?" said a young man.

The harshness of the fluorescent lighting accentuated his rosacea cheeks. His green name tag spelled Tyler. Does Tyler need to hear the heart ache this trek to find myself has produced? I haven't found the recipe for my malaise, not here, not anywhere. A dirty, dull penny laid on the floor at Tyler's foot. No relief from the pesticide glowing produce. The glass cases filled with meat and chicken are saturated with hormones and reek of antibiotics. The magazines racks hold headlines of negativity, innuendos, and lies. What can I eat to remove the rancid taste in my life? I look for something healthy to nurture me, only to find rows of bright colored boxes and bags holding toxic truths.

"No, I haven't found what I am looking for," I said.

CAROL ANNE SMART

SPILT MILK
She curled my hair
I sat perfectly still in the chair
I felt warm inside
The way I used to feel when Nana held me
When I was a little girl
The way I never felt with Mother
I had to work too hard to get Mother's love
It went away too easily
If I spilled the milk
Or didn't make my bed just right
So, I learned not to spill the milk
And how to make the bed without wrinkles
How to iron
How to curl her hair
Just to feel that warm feeling

I felt it most when she read to me
She loved doing that
I would sit right next to her
And learn the words
Just one more story, Mommy, please
I didn't want the story to end

Or the moment

I swore when I had children
I wouldn't get so upset over spilt milk

I didn't have children

STRAY MEN
My sister picked up stray cats
She would bring them home
Fill the saucer with milk
She would meet me at the door
With sad round eyes and a sheepish smile
She would say
Can we keep this kitten
He needs a good home

I picked up stray men
Always intelligent
Usually charming
Complicated
Down on their luck
Needing assistance

The world wasn't treating him right
His boss didn't like him
His wife didn't understand him

The exact words my father said to me
When he came into my bed
As I grew to the age of twelve

THE CAMEL
Lone light on a hill like the lone light of the ranch house
Pure darkness all around except its solitary light
Solitary existence, five miles from town
There were mornings when I couldn't talk
I sat on my bed, rocking back and forth, fast then slow
Knees tucked under my chin, hands clutching arms
Arms and legs with bruises, colors revealing their age
Only Giant Panda Bear, his large brown eyes
With infinite black pupils, witnessed it all
But the stars came out every night
I could see them through my bedroom window
When he didn't block the view
Blue chenille curtains that I wouldn't close
If the moon shone, I would have a warning light
Maybe a siren would protect me
Like the sirens that protected Mother
From the Buzz Bombs in London
I'll stir up a hornet's nest this time, hornets swarming
Preparing to attack their prey, never a lone soldier
His decorated R.A.F. uniform, covered with tissue
Placed in the cedar chest at the foot of their bed

The embroidered multi-colored bars sewn on green cloth
A symbol of all the missions he had flown
His promotion to Lieutenant Colonel in the US Airforce
The Spitfires flew in my mind
His plane was decorated with an Angel
She had large round breasts like Mommy
The ones he couldn't wait for me to have
It was a car that took me away

I couldn't wait for the plane that would come years later
To Jerusalem at the foot of the Mount of Olives
In the Garden of Gethsemane
Observing one square mile holding
Religion's most holy sites
The Wailing Wall of King David's Temple
The Muslim Mosque with its Golden Dome
The Church of the Holy Sepulcher
God in the form of a camel
Wise brown eyes, black pupils, seeing all, observing silently

BONNIE SOLOMAN

ENOUGH OF THIS PUSSYFOOTING AROUND
Enough of this Pussyfooting Around.
You are not the result of a Half-Hearted Bang.
The Universe didn't ask to dip a toe
in the Water of Life,
Or lease Existence for a one-month trial.
It didn't shrug off Creation as a Good Idea
But Too Tricky to Take Seriously.
It didn't listen to the Haters
Who coldly questioned its work experience?
No.
It exploded in their faces,
It made space and time and gravity and stars
And atmospheres and dinosaurs and hybrid cars
And You—
A being with the capacity to Love
As fully and fiercely as the unbridled
YES
That set the Universe in motion.
Every breath you take is a sacred testament
To the mind-blowing fact that anything exists at all.
You are Epic.
So, please,
Enough of this Pussyfooting Around.

HEADSHOTS
I want to see my true nature,
So, I ask God to take my picture.
I'll do it, she says, *but I'm busy* and *I don't come cheap.*
We make a deal on PayPal and head to her studio.

There's a stool and a camera and a lot of White Light.
I face the camera with my Good Side
And give Her my best smile,
The one that gets me laid and convinces other people
To see things My Way.
God turns on the Fog Machine and tells me to relax.
Be natural.
I breathe in a thick cloud of Something Unpleasant
And realize that she's gassing me with Truth.
I fall off the stool and curl into a ball
But God makes me lie flat so the energy flows freely.
Then she gets behind the camera.
Click.
Oh fuck, it's toomuchtoomuchtoomuch.
I feel everything that ever was. Is. Will be. Won't be.
All at once.
I lose my mind as if it was my car keys,
But I can't find it in any of the Usual Places,
So, I look to God for mercy.
She changes the aperture…and splays open my soul.
I am. Utterly. Infinitely. Over. Exposed.
And then it happens: I Let Go.
It comes out of every orifice.
An epic release of All That Is Not Me,
Otherwise known as the Stuff That Is Not Love.
When it's over, I ache with Aliveness.
And bask in the simplicity of Being.
I sit up, and God hands me a Polaroid.
It's blank.
I start to giggle. So, does She.
Soon we're doubled over, busting a gut
In deference to The Mystery,
In celebration of The Journey,
And all the sacred stops for photo ops along the way.

REAL MAGIC
I'm over swords and sorcery.
I'm no longer into superheroes
Who use violence to solve problems.
Don't *even* get me started on the Stage Magicians
Who've taken over television
And kept us so in fear of the State of the World
That we've forgotten we are actually
Miracles in Motion
With an infinite capacity to create and evolve.
You want to know what turns me on?
Real Magic.
Connection. Vulnerability.
The courage it takes to Be Yourself.
The belly laugh that heals The Day from Hell.
The wave of pleasure that explodes from my jaw
When I let my head go at dance or speak from my soul.
Passion. Presence.
The willingness to Keep Showing Up.

The pain that eventually transmutes into poetry.
The impulse that urges the Dude in the Headphones
To talk to the Lonely Old Man at the bus stop.
The glimpse in the mirror that shocks
The Middle-Aged Woman into realizing that
She finally loves her body.
Intention. Compassion.
The boldness to Be Messy, to Fuck Up—
And the grace to learn from our mistakes.
The moment we look one another in the eye
And Tell the Hard Truth
Even and especially when we think it will break us.
You want to know what turns me on?
The hope in the heart of the Ordinary Human,
Which staunchly refuses to stop beating love
No matter how many transgressions it's endured.
We are magic, my friends—
Real Magic.
And we can rise above the Smoke and Mirrors
To choose the world we want to live in.

CHRISTINE SPAUKA CONNER

A FLACCID JESUS

Carlos dressed in white Lacoste Polo shirts and slightly baggy jeans, long before they were a thing. He wore his black curly hair unkempt. He always looked somewhat sloppy—a persona held together by a green crocodile above his heart and a silver belt buckle above his groin.

He owned Bar Playa in Malaga. The only thing that could hint a smudge of self care or indicate a vanity of sorts, was the pitch-black eyeliner he used along his lower eye lids. Carlos looked like a mix out of the Spanish crooner Julio Iglesias and Freddie Mercury, the gay lead singer from Queen. Actually, at that time, every Spaniard between the age of 20 and 70 looked like a mix of Julio Iglesias with some other male—at least to me. My running joke-answer, when someone asked me why I came to Spain, was always: I'm here to meet Julio Iglesias. In fact, it wasn't a joke. I knew all the lyrics to all of Julio's songs. They were not as trivial as one might think, poetic ballads really, somewhere in between a Hallmark card and Rilke. I liked his exaggerated accent his extreme "SH" sound instead of a true Castilian "J," *shega* instead of *jega*. In Spain they made fun of him because of that. It sounded to the Spanish ear like a speech impediment—not to mine. To me they were poetry. Carlos' older brother Roberto looked like Julio Iglesias combined with George Clooney. He had somewhat of a statesman appearance, he owned a famous restaurant in Marbella, had a young wife, a beauty queen from Madrid, a new baby and drove a red Porsche 911. Carlos drove a green Volvo, was forced by his father into a marriage with the first girl he got pregnant. She was from a pueblo in the mountains and looked more like ham and potatoes, especially when next to Roberto's long-legged Miss Spain. She had come for work to the Costa del Sol and ended up as a waitress in Carlos' restaurant. By the time I met him she was in her third pregnancy and he on his hundreds something fuck affair with a blonde Dutch, German, or English tourist. Even though the English were not so popular, not that they were not willing, they were, believe me, but the Dutch and German were prettier and mostly blonde. Trophy fucks, we called them, paraded by their machos along the beach promenade as if at a car show. Shiny and new. Hi, this is Bettina! Did you meet Mareike? The relationships were mutual. The girls weren't victims. A Julio look-a-like on your side for a couple of weeks provided a full Spanish emersion program.

Carlos probably had contracted AIDS by that time but didn't know it yet. The AIDS epidemic was at full swing in the beginning of the nineties. But nobody cared. I didn't either. With each passing year and after each OBGYN check up. I high-fived myself. Made it! I never was a trophy fuck. Not that I didn't have my share of "Costa-Fun" but I chose wisely. I liked Chino, yes, chino like Chinese, a friend of Carlos and Roberto. He looked like the perfect combo of my crooner Julio and Benicio del Torro. He was from Valladolid, in the middle of the country. They sometimes look like that there, Carlos told me.

We were all out that night. On Cocktails of JB—Jota B—Cocaine and Chocolate—the dry weed from the gypsies, that looks like beef jerky. I kind of was with Chino, but flirted with anyone who looked like Julio, as if it was my private manifest destiny. My own westward journey. Chino was a mild-mannered son of a wealthy builder overseeing a new hotel project on the coast. He drove me home that night. We kissed lightly goodbye in front of my house.

Later in my bed, I could hear the waves crashing against the beach. My lullaby. I never lived that close to the beach again.

Bang! Bang! Bang! I heard a loud pounding against the door of my bungalow. I wasn't afraid as usual, because I was drunk and stoned. I actually made sure that I was one or the other every night in order not to be scared alone in my little house. The nights I wasn't intoxicated enough I slept with a butcher knife underneath my pillow. I made my way down the creaking stairs. When I heard: Christina, Christina, abre, abre! I thought I recognized Carlos' voice. Also, the silhouette I saw through my milk glass door indicated my friend. I opened the door. Then everything was very quick, a blur of black unkempt hair, teamos, baggy jeans, clinking belt buckle—waves crashing hard. I can't remember if I screamed. I probably did, but it was like in those dreams where you scream and scream but you don't have a voice. And nobody hears you. Nobody comes to save you. Nobody wants you. Nobody needs you. Nobody likes you. Nobody cares. Nobody. Nobody. Nobody.

I just know I kicked and kicked and kicked. Then everything was still. He was gone. And in my hand, I held a golden necklace with a cross and a tiny Jesus hanging—flaccid. The Mediterranean Sea drowned my crying with her lullaby.

The next morning, I went to Bar Playa. Carlos, held together by the green crocodile and the silver belt buckle, was in a conversation behind the bar with his father, who did not look like a Julio Iglesias clone. Carlos didn't anymore either. I slammed the flaccid Jesus on the counter and said: Never again.

FRAN SUTTON-WILLIAMS

THEY CROSSED THE RIVER
–because the slaves were so happy...

Lord, she was so tired. They'd been runnin' all night. She was glad for the snow at first, she thought it would cover their tracks and make it hard for the dogs to find them, but they kept comin'. She thanked Jesus that the draught she'd been givin' Sweets caused her to sleep all this while. There was no time for her to stop and put the baby to her breast. The boys were hungry. Wendall started to cry from the hunger but she told him he would have to be a big boy like Gerald, so he stopped. He'd been quiet since then and Gerald hadn't made a sound in hours. They were good boys though Ada told the Massa otherwise hoping he would leave them be, but he didn't. He told her they were going to be sold. He said she could keep Sweets until she didn't need Ada's breast milk, but then she would have to go as well. Sweets being half-white and female, she would fetch a good price. He said Ada should be happy for Sweets, she was going to grow up to be a house slave, no working the fields like Ada did. Gram Pritchard told Ada she wouldn't get with child if she had one at her breast, but she was wrong. Massa Wolfe went to Ada, though Gram had told him to wait until Ada was healed from birthin' Sweets, but he didn't wait, and he brought friends. That day she knew, she felt the quickening and knew there was another child in her belly. That was when it came upon her to take the children and run. There was freedom on the other side of the river and Sunshine had whispered to Ada that there was a man who would help them cross near where the river splits if they came to him at night. He would take anything as payment and Ada took the only thing of value in the barn—the knife made for skinnin' the game when it was brought home. She'd heard the men say that it was made of steel. That and a heel of bread and a piece of salt pork were all they had to their names. It wasn't that far to the river, but she was so tired, and the dogs were right behind them. They wouldn't make it to the river and now there's blood in the snow, her blood in the snow. She'd made sure they would all cross the river together...

#

Chaz Whiggins had been chasing runaway slaves for years. Some fought at the end, but they all quieted under the lash. This time, they were already quiet when he rode into the clearing and found blood in the snow. That damned woman had took the lives of her three children! How unnatural was that? It just showed how they were not human, the nigras. No mother would treat her children so. Take her own life, yes, but she could have left the children. They were meant to be sold. Now Chaz would have to go back to Mister Wolfe and tell him they were all lost. He was not going to get his money after all. None of them was gonna get paid.

BRYNN THAYER

REMINDERS

I need to buy some new clothes to wear while I'm in the hospital, she says.

I didn't know you were going to the hospital? I say. What's wrong?

Always be prepared. I wanna look good while I'm at the hospital, she says. I need to find a couple of quilted bed jackets.

Okay, I say. I'll look online.

No. I want to get them at Neiman's—soft pastels.

I don't think they make them anymore, Mom.

That's impossible, she says. A woman can live without a man but she can't live without a satin bed jacket.

Mom is the OG of her bridge club. Meets every other Tuesday. Bad Momma's, they call themselves. In 1951, they began with six tables of hot housewives dressed to the nines and one alternate. Drink wine, play cards, eat lavish lunch, drink wine, play cards, eat fancy hors d'oeuvres, drink wine, play cards, rinse and repeat, all day long. Notorious competitors, they were. All the women in town wanted membership into Bad Momma's. An outsider had to pray that a member either move or die to be considered for the coveted spot. A grueling bridge tournament was held to determine the best candidate. It was rumored that two women committed suicide when they found out they weren't good enough to join the club. These days the Bad Momma's are down to three-quarters of a table. They have trouble getting a substitute and bring their lunches in brown paper bags. But they play on, keeping the game alive for the dearly departed. Average age—95.

I found a small easel, she says, so I'm going to put it in the bathroom and display a different picture on it every week. I'll call it—Picture of the Week. It'll brighten up my bathroom, she says. Last week it was a picture of you in that navy checkered jumper when you were two, this week it was you around 13 sitting on Ginger at the Ft. Worth horse show. And this morning, she says, I found a picture of you from your first wedding minus the husband. But I want you to know that you might not always be the picture of the week.

That's fine, Mom.

I want to remind you of a couple of things, she says. Do you have a pencil?

Number One: If you're trying on a dress with a zipper, be sure to sit in it before you buy it.

Number Two: There's no need for the funeral home to bathe me before the cremation. I will have had my bath in the morning, and I'd prefer no one sees me naked.

Number Three: Keep a little mystery in your marriage, dear.

Number Four: Let go of grudges. Grudges put weight on, and those pounds are hard to get off once they latch on to the thighs.

Number Five: Get my gal at the beauty shop to come over to do my hair when you're sure I'm dead. She said she would. I've already paid her. Tip included.

Number Six: Remember that love is the only way.

Number Seven: My jewelry is hidden in a wooden box behind the *Atlas* on the lower shelf in the library. What number am I on?

Number Three: Always write thank you notes with pen and paper. Purchase high thread count sheets. Please don't spend anymore time ironing. That's why they invented dry cleaners. I've loved being your mother.

She twisted her hands. And took a breath.

VACHINE

MISSION

I love the smell of napalm in the morning.
–Robert Duvall, *Apocalypse Now*

I didn't write Gook on the napalm canister.
I didn't fasten the ordinance under-wing of the A-7.
I didn't fire the catapult that flung the fighter off the Hawk.
I didn't release the Gook bomb over Trang Bang.
I didn't splash jellied gasoline
O n Phan Thị Kim Phúc OOnt.
I did my best to ensure spare parts for Corsair's flight.
I did see that picture a girl running from her village.
I did see that she was screaming, skin on fire.
I did know Gook spoke for the mission.
I did know no one spoke for the burning child.
I now know that running girl has a name.

REQUIEM

Well, I went to Al's memorial today at Thursday, Brentwood. Must have been say over 1,200 people there, knew many from AA, a lot to revere a guy like that Mexican-Irish guy from San Gabriel. We sat silent except to laugh or groan. The throng was still for two full hours, no schpilkes, sat, cried, laughed.

The Memorialists on stage told stories of crazy stunts Al pulled on the mourner like calling Al in desperation because rent was due, caller had no money to make rent. Al asked when the rent was due, the answer was in three weeks.

Al asked, "Do you have a place to sleep until then? Is there food in your frig? If yes, we'll talk later."

Those stories comforted me. I worry over too many nothings myself. I've known these AAs thirty years, they've become wrinkled, old looking, and fat, like me. The years of gravity have pulled my tight spots down so they're hangy-downs now, but I am still above ground.

Some of the folks I loved along the way killed themselves hanging, gluttony, or pistol. It's what happens, 85% that come in go out, get drunk, and die, but life is so nice in the sanctuary of 1,200 sober liars, cheats, thieves, sluts—my people. You can't put one over on us because, as a group, we have committed all the felonies there are. We've done it all and that's why it's so easy to love us, we laugh at bad shit happening, because we survived our own selves, now have a sober life worth living.

I am grateful daily I didn't blow out my brains like I was planning, park my Camry on the wrong side of Topanga, near a little gulch covered with green leafy vegetation hiding the culvert beneath, so when trigger of .45 against my head pulled, momentum would push my slack bones through greenery into the culvert, no one would know cadaver was there until they investigated my illegally parked car, rummaged through the bushes. At least it would be easy to retrieve my remains, slide onto coroner's gurney, motor silently to the morgue.

See, that's all I thought about for two years, seeking solace from the unending Asian War I brought home, before being admitted for treatment to UCLA 6 West. In the Day Room, we enjoyed each other's company, purgers, cutters, and sordid near suicides. I provided evidence of disposition of all my guns so the Docs would treat me.

Fell in love with Amanda, an over-doser from lockup, recently released to our Day Room, child taken away by County Fosters. I cried over her fate. She just wanted to be gone like me. We had craft time together afternoons. You could finger-paint, mold a clay bunny, or whatever else, I wrote poems, when compared with older work, read more like suicide notes, took poetry lessons as Aftercare. No gifts on Graduation day, the wife visited, wanted a divorce, said she's done with PTSD men.

MAUREEN VAUGHAN

FAMED OUT

Last year, my friend, Elizabeth, drowned when she accidentally drove her car into a stream in Southern California on her way to commit suicide in Durango, Mexico. Elizabeth's husband, a wonderful, sensitive professor, had called me in great distress a few days earlier to tell me that his bipolar wife had stopped taking her meds and had taken off in the car, screaming she was heading to Durango. This caused me great fear as Elizabeth's mother, a once semi-famous actress in the days of the early talkies, had co-starred with John Wayne in a movie filmed in Durango and she had fallen from a cliff in the movie. Now, I am heartsick because I think I saw this coming but did nothing to stop it. But what could I have done? I don't know. Elizabeth was a terrible actress, but her entire life was spent trying to become a star. No one, including me, had the heart to tell her she just wasn't any good. Even more than 50 years ago when we were still in our teens, and unlike now when teachers and elders were generally not afraid to tell you that you were untalented or not capable of certain endeavors, something about Elizabeth kept us from telling her the truth. She couldn't sing, dance, or act worth beans. But she wanted stardom and a career so badly—she worked so hard, she prayed so hard, she dreamt so hard—no one close to her had the heart to tell her she stunk. But I guess she realized this herself—at the age of 21, she was found by policemen throwing mud on herself in a ditch. She was diagnosed as manic-depressive, now known as bipolar, and given lithium. When taking lithium, Elizabeth managed to live a fairly normal life; she became an English teacher and in her early forties met and married Michael, a calm, intelligent man. But like all of us who loved her, he too encouraged her to go on her always unsuccessful auditions and participate in her endless dreadful showcases.

A few weeks before her death, I called Elizabeth to congratulate her on the teaching award she had received from the community college where she worked.

"Oh, yeah, thanks," said Elizabeth, "but Louise, I just re-watched that old John Wayne movie that Mom was in. It was so good! I really identified with her character. I would have been great in that film."

A residual payment lay on my bed. My iPhone was heavy in my hand.

"Elizabeth," I answered, "that part would have made you a star."

DAVID WILZIG

THE BLACK DOT

There's a back dot atop my left hand
27 bones unaffected in their precise movement
by that black dot, a circle the size of a hand rolled cig
but my badge, placed there at the 1st Battle of my Roses.

The longest battle-day—over 10 hours,
drip, drip, slowly, then rapid heartbeat, d.t's, shakes,
cold frigid cold, unwarned by blankets.
Unhorsed, I cried: "more, please more blankets" and
they eased the drugs slowly, slowly
then Maxwellian, drip, drip to the last drop
the fluids attacked...whom? what? Where?

Russian like, I engage a daily war
of Red and White armies not knowing, even now
not knowing whether I favor the Russian Red Army
or the White Army.
I have a lovely LP of the Russian Red Army singing.
I know about Snow White, white and even yellow snow.

A singular drop of water in a pool of blood.
Life-force flowing ebbs into a wan pink,
spreading slowly sunset into its pond...
The War of Leukocytes—G-d what an ugly word.
I had to check its spelling—white blood cells
from the Greek leucos, clear, white.

I shall be white lain on a white chrome table
and the leucos shall have won.
I's rather they were spelled with a "d"—lewd,
struck deep in my throat.

Lances drawn these white soldiers posted.
Up and down thoracically.
Jousting here, cutting there, causing an itch,
developing a cough to be visited by doctors in white.

A white knight appeared—as is required for the joust.
A nobleman, with his own horse and, at the signal
a sound I never did hear until the coughing
was uncontrollable—he'd ride with lance and shield
along the right side of my throats dividing bar.

I have read that only three lances were permitted,
once shattered, the tourney was over.
My lances were January, February and March,
for by early April, the men in white jackets
and, ultimately the oversized Latina
who drew $28 of my blood gently carried

to the white doctor who said,
"My noble friend, you have cancer."

MAKE WAY FOR BIG PRICKS

In the guise of science, hah!
Not unlike my prepubescent perusals
of *National Geographic*,
the old Gray Lady reports
that some duck cocks, yes, they used
the word phallus,
but cock it is—
can grow as long as a duck's body.
What a Johnson that would be!

Not *Hustler* but the *New York Times*.

How often-coated with sweat,
caked with whatever,
I'd roll over hiding my shriveled cock,
dreaming, of what? Now, I know
dreaming that I could turn into
a Mellers Duck from Madagascar
and it's not like I haven't visited Madagascar.
I did and it's not like I didn't need
extreme genitals, I did—not easy
satisfying a Doctor Without Borders

Thankfully the old Gray Lady advises
and, I for one, believe everything in her paper
that we—now I relate to the noble mallard
are big pricks only
to satisfy the extremity of a cavernous pussy—
of a fellow duck, wood, teal, or Muscovy.
I'm uncertain if ducks have pussies or vaginas,
but I am delighted to report to all those ex'es
that I was right.
They were the cause of my prickliness.

New meaning to a reading
of "Make Way for Ducklings."

ISAAC WORSTEL-RUBIN

I AM TRASH

5 I hid behind the curtains in my parents' room while they weren't there. It was dark. "My parents don't love me," said the voice in my head. I was scared half to death by the voice in my head trying to convince me my parents didn't love me. I struggled against it. Struggled hard. The room was well lit, but the curtains were dark and there was a small box of matches on the table just around the edge of the curtains. I

was an innocent child, I didn't know any better. Stuck in the curtains—there was only darkness. I was wearing a white shirt with a red firetruck on it. It was dark and I couldn't figure out how to turn on the light in my heart. I stopped struggling. I lit myself on fire and burned from then on. I'm trash, therefore worthless.

18 I met my next love and told her I would never date or commit to her because relationships don't make sense. It was October 1st or 2nd or so, and there was a party, so naturally I was wearing nothing but boxers and covered in baby oil. There was porn all over the walls. I was drunk as could be—I don't even remember how drunk. All I remember is this: I looked up. There she was. Brunette goddess in a blue dress with tiny sunflowers all over it. She looked like she was shy, but she knew everything. I can't describe how I felt because that's how I felt about seeing her. The shy girl looked right at me—eye to eye. A ripped-up piece of porn was on the floor and a half a cigarette. We were in a colonial house. We danced. I kissed her on the neck. She said, "I have a boyfriend!" She left. The next night she came back. "I broke up with my boyfriend." Next thing I knew we were in my bed. Next thing I knew, we were in my bed all the time. Then her bed. But we still weren't dating. Relationships don't make sense. I'm trash.

19 I painted my first painting—a man screaming just like the Pope, with a five-pronged tongue, ripping his brains out his skull with his own hand. My second love fell in love with me, but I didn't notice and when I realized I loved her I asked her to come over and I told her I loved her—she said I didn't. On her way over, a friend of hers had just told her I fucked another girl. She didn't think we were exclusive, but she loved me anyway, so it hurt her bad enough. From then on, she thought she was trash. I didn't realize how much she hated herself until I was 20. The girl I fucked lost her mind trying to interpret the meaning of my words when I told her I was done. She committed herself to the ward and I didn't see her for three years. Three months after she went crazy, my second love left me for the first time. I'd realized I had PTSD from my first relationship. She said she was depressed. She said she'd always had it but looking back I can tell it was exacerbated by what I did to her. She still came to see me whenever she wanted. She carried a notebook. I asked what it was, she said it was lists. I liked that. I'd relax so she could be however she was without any pressure. After two months of being herself, who she never wasn't, she broke down and smiled again and it caused a thunderstorm. I told her I loved her. She believed it now. Lightning cracked as she whispered, "I love you, too." Then she smiled and cried and smiled more and she couldn't stop saying it. "I love you. I love you. I love you. I love you. I love you." She said she'd be here from now on and a week after that she'd forgotten and left the second time. The next time I saw her she had a snake wrapped around her waist. We got back together a third time, but we broke up a fourth because of the damage I did to her. She showed me everything about love and then evaporated. After the first time, she thought she was trash. When she told me, I saw I wasn't, but I didn't believe it. We got back together but now she didn't want to call it that because she told me relationships don't make sense. She thought she was trash, therefore worthless. One day my love opened her notebook to write a grocery list. As she flipped through the pages, I saw what she wrote, in all caps, next to the catalog she made that I was seeing for the first time, too—it was her daily weight with some notes next to it. The notes read: "YOU'RE FAT. KILL YOURSELF." She wasn't. She was beautiful, perfect, and good in every way. I'm not just saying that. Six months later she got so depressed, she forgot who I was. I was right there when it happened. I leaned to kiss her on the cheek. I was wearing sweatpants. There was a movie paused—*Royal Tenenbaums*. The perfect goddess who thought she should kill herself was wearing a white shirt. There was a strawberry in the carton. It was humid. I had a bunch of mosquito bites. I had gone to a party and had no service. When she got there, I wasn't there—but we'd figured it out. Not a good start but it shouldn't have been what it became. She shied away and asked me why I was treating her like we were in love. I said because we are and have been for the past two years. She said, "No. We're friends but that's it." The confusion was too much for me. She saw I was confused and thought I was crazy. Then I thought maybe I was crazy. Maybe this was the schizophrenia setting in. Holy shit. A week after she'd ran out of the house, got in her car, and sped away, all. I lay in bed trying to rip my brains out of my skull as I realized I couldn't help her understand that she's good—she's okay, she's not fucked up, not trash, not worthless. She's enough—she's more than enough. She thought me how to love. She was never able to receive it. That's my fault. I thought I was trash. Clutching my reality in my hands, I realized every single person would have to realize they're good and perfect in order not to perpetuate the fuckedupness. We torture ourselves and others by feeling fucked up. It's heartbreaking. How can anyone help anyone else feel the way others know they are? At some point a friend of mine commented on this period of my life saying "I've never seen anyone love someone the way you loved her." Later she told me it made her question her own concept of love and she had some kind of crisis about it.

21 We hadn't gotten back together again but were still talking. She started cutting herself. One day she drank a jug of wine in the bathtub and cut too deep. The last time I saw her, she said "I'm leaving, and I don't know what I'm going to do." I never saw her again. She wanted to be an architect. They say a house is a soul and mine was immolated just by seeing the design of hers. No more trash in or around. I wanted the whole world to be like that. Since then I never stopped wanting that. *Burn it all. Burn it all. For everyone.*

Then I realized, if you look at trash—really look—just look—and watch—start to see—wait for it—eventually… spontaneous combustion.

KERSTIN ZILM

BODY OF LOVE

May smoldering coal sycamores
Line your thorny paths
And meadows bereft of light.
May rainbow marine layers
Arch from translucent skin
To old bones freedom,
Smiling.

May boiling water burn your hands.
May raging desire tear the flesh off your nails.
May you scream in your dreams,
Sword stuck in your throat,
Begging for someone to help,
To bend down, to surrender with you,
To love you in vain.

May you shower in molten gold.
May you cover your layers of flesh in money lava.
May you find you're alone—
Always.

May you tear your heart from your chest.
May you carry beating blood in the palms of your hand.
May you offer it to the flames
Of ancient pyramids and sacred wood.
May you serve your soul on platters of rubies
and diamonds
At banquets to Queens and Kings
Only to find thieves
Behind their elaborate masks of Hollywood smiles—
Their perfumed disgust.

May you stand naked between oak trees and pines,
Hunters advancing fast,
Arrows and rifles pointed at you,
Bloodhounds following the scent of your sweat.
May you hunch
Under stares of lions and three-headed deers
Until you are totally bare.

Then stand up,
Let go of that armor.
Let maggots and moist leaves
Fall off your skin.
Stretch

Beauty and grace.
Expose the animal that you are,
Scars on your face,
Coal on your skin,
Invincible.

Stomp your feet through cold dirt
Until earth's magma boils the blood in your veins
Fills your fingertips.

Let the roar from your loins move cloud mountains,
Send a shiver through the planet,
Ring into the universe,
Push off the ground.
Spread your arms,
Rule the world.

Find companions of all shapes and forms
From ashes beneath you will grow
Flowers and creeks,
Music and stillness,
Oceans, valleys and hills.

Know that your wings,
Your beaten flesh,
You'd skinned heart,
Your burning blood,
Are your body
With nothing to spare,
Nothing to receive,
Nothing to give,
But love.

JAMES ZUKIN

THE BABYSITTER FROM HELL
the ad lurked in the *Neighborhood Shopper*
the local weekly throw-away paper
"babysitter required for two boys
please send us your references"

and soon came victim number nine
our favorite sport was to begin again
it's *VEX THE SITTER* time!

the monster with sensible shoes
enters our happy home shuffling
to us all sitters were sent by the devil
our parents rush out she remains
inspects her new lair with a smile
hiding her serpent's tongue
her lips shine bright as fresh blood

when her webbed fingers spread
like a spider I knew our lives
were in danger we had to act fast

my brother the gymnast had a routine
I throw him high into the air
he grabs the chandelier
twists around and takes aim
to land on the babysitter feet first

she did not move…
we were in a state of shock
was that a wink?
we could not tell…

NEWBRIDGENEVERUSEDNOWCLOSED
aroadstopsatabridgestopsandwaitsforrainfall
thebridgeteasestheroadinmeetingtheroad
entersthebridgeafterashortcourtshipfeaturing
burntrubbertheroadproposesthebridgeaccepts
andclosestocarsringofconcretehoneymoon
virtualtheylivedhappilyeverafterofcourseher
cablesweretiedmanyyearsagotheyarethinkingof
adoptingayoungchinesesuspensionbridgenamed
wontonmaritalmodestyrequiresacoveringthe
roadplansabigsurprise!beforethebigdayasecond
deckwascompleteandopenthemayorcut
theribbonwhentheyclosed.

A DANCER'S LIFE
I.
I watch my daughter
ballet becomes her
infuses her young face
with passion

she challenges gravity
as she flies without a care
she awaits the ovations
the stage spotlights
ingénue in the wings

II.
I fear for my daughter
that she will become a tragedian
never to ring down the curtains
as a prima ballerina

her short career danced in pain
toe shoes hiding blood stains
her face a mask agony never revealed
stress fractures then ankle destruction
a sense of allegro soon forgotten

break slow
break slow
heal toe
heal toe

III.
a father stands alone at the stage door
with flowers

Drawing: Richard Gayler

FEATURING:
RICHARD GAYLER
BAZ HERE
URBAN POSSIBILITIES

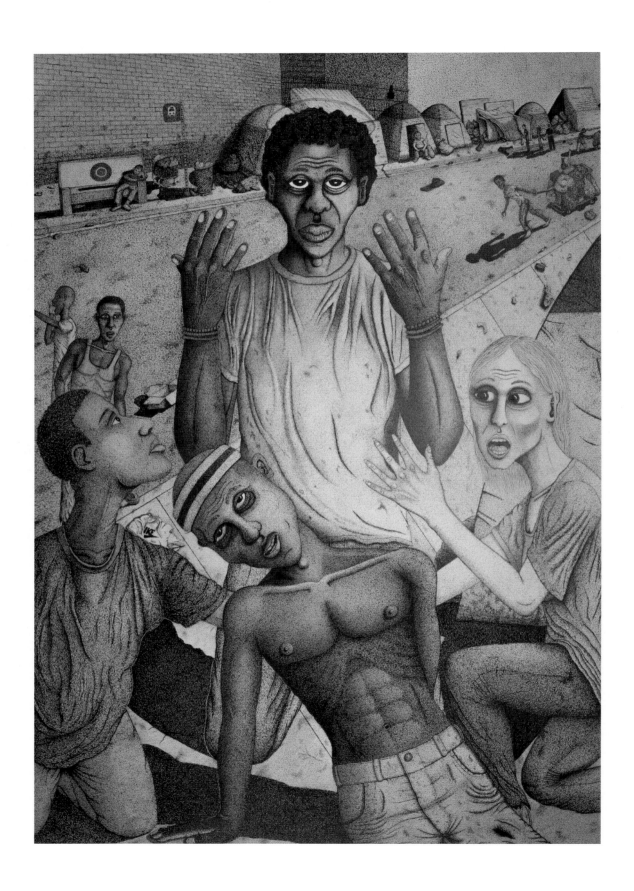

Richard Gayler is a Los Angeles born, self-taught artist. He has worked using different mediums over the years, including assemblage, painting, encaustic, photography, and collage. His current focus is on drawing, with an emphasis on using his own style of stippling. His artwork is inspired by his experiences and (at times, satirical) observations of the complicated times in which we live. He is trying to engage viewers on topics such as homelessness, consumerism, pollution, ecology, and activism. He tries to present the viewer with alternative themes, situations, or views that may challenge their beliefs and ideas. The ultimate goal is to inspire viewers to examine their lives and choices with new perspectives in mind.

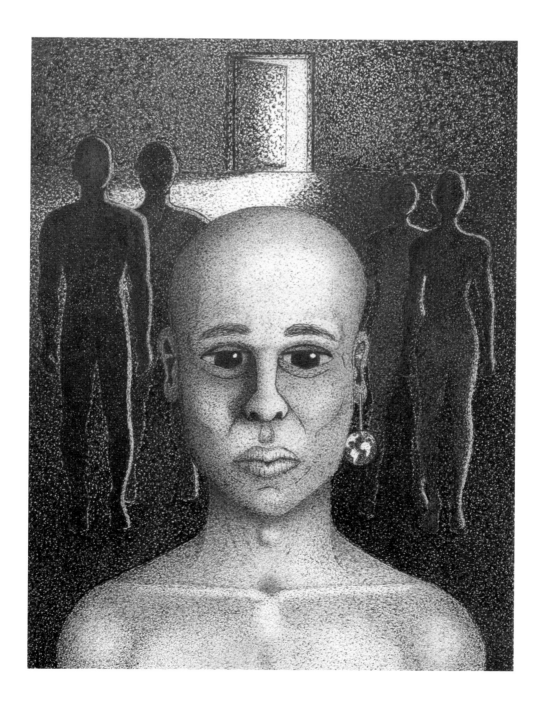

After thousands of years of his listening to complaints about the heat, tired of being universally labeled as an enabler, and feeling burned out, he finally accepted the inevitable and proceeded to collapse upon himself.

WHITE ON WHITE

Kean O'Brien in Conversation with Baz Here

originally published in FAYN Issue 08

KEAN O'BRIEN:

How did you get to this place in your practice where you began examining the themes of white privilege, queerness, and masculinity? Looking back at your previous work I can see you are using your body as subject in similar ways, but these images have a much more political lens than your other work.

BAZ HERE:

Before this series, my work was more focused on my own personal journey and trauma from having to disidentify from heteronormative culture. The work was often criticized as hermetic, by having no real access point. I was less concerned with the way the work might be perceived and thinking more about my relationship with my queerness and the religion I was raised to believe in. In my work, *The Temptation of St. Baz*, I was searching for a way to reinvent the savior archetype through the use of my body and religious iconography. This neo-savior became my sexuality and my naked body. The symbols of gay male sex culture became the tools of my healing. Once I started thinking about myself as a part of something larger (the gay community) and realizing the impact my work could make, I started to think about what it means to have white male privilege.

KO:

What do you mean by "white male privilege?"

BH:

White male privilege or Whiteness as being a construct that is inherently invested in racism... I'm only beginning to understand the scope of how deeply my white privilege permeates throughout my body and my daily life. I have always had friends, lovers, and sexual partners that were POC (people of color) so I felt I was the opposite of racist. I bought into the neoliberal idea that I did not see race. I was in this ambiguous region somewhere between ignorance and gay apathy. At some point, I decided to become more observant of people's behavior, and more specifically, the contrast of how people treated me vs. people of color I know. I saw just how much less policed I am and how much greater access I have to opportunities, all because I have white skin.

KO:

The way your body interacts with these projections of men seems to me to represent vulnerability and a quest for arousal. How are you thinking about your body in these images? Can you speak to the metaphor that the projected images hold?

BH:

I am naked often in my work, but I don't consider that being vulnerable. A lot of the time I feel I'm using my nakedness as a symbol of power. However, in this series, I chose to connect with the submissive side of myself by performing poses where I felt exposed and unprotected — positioned to give away control. In order to understand the abundance of privilege that I hold, I needed to form a union (via their — white cis men of historical power — image projected onto my body) with the toxic masculine oppressive white supremacy that I abhor. I had to sit with

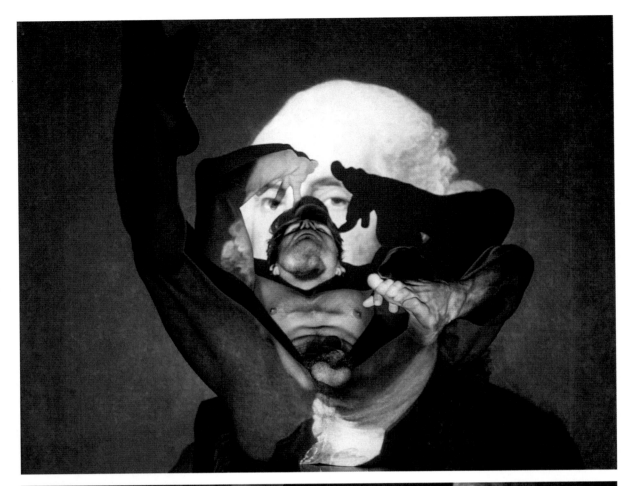

my own resentment of that dominant archetype (straight white masculinity) as a white gay male, and my pathway was through sexual exploration. I needed to get fucked, and I had to be the bottom.

The projection of the powerful white man onto my skin acts as not exactly a metaphor, but as a signifier to my inability to shed my skin. No matter how much I can change within, I will always be a visual representation of whiteness.

I wanted to project infamous white male leaders onto my body, and seek out grandiose paintings of them — to me, if they had that kind of painting made of themselves, they were subscribing to their own narcissism and relationship with power (the monarchical tradition). I knew that the portraits would then distort as they wrapped around my body, but the result was surprising. I started to really play with this amalgamation of my body and their faces and what it meant for their eyes, nose, and mouth to touch my penis, my butt, my naked body. For a moment I could try and imagine what it felt like to have the power these men had.

KO:

What are your current projects?

BH:

I'm finding my voice as a white male artist in an art world landscape that is already over-occupied by white artists. I'd like to use my privilege to help pushback against the white supremacist's hetero capitalist patriarchy and it's instruments of oppression. I know that I must make art, but I am spending most of my time in meditation and research and investing in my growth in compassion… and smothering my white ego.

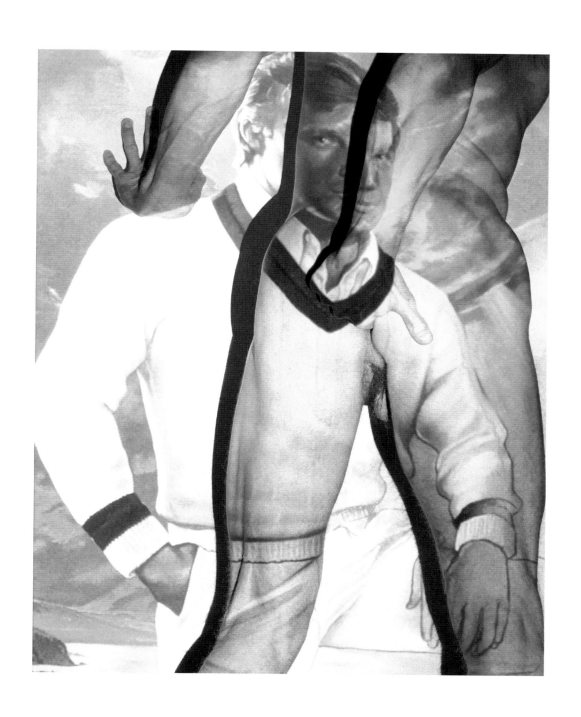

INNER CITY ALCHEMY

By Eyvette Jones-Johnson
Executive Director, Urban Possibilities

In the deepest caverns of Los Angeles, and in its most unlikely places, there is infinite treasure. Growing exponentially over time, spreading to every corner of the county, lining the routes we travel to work and play. Yet if treasure is there, why can't we see it?

The answer lies in perception. Just as magicians make us see a woman sawed in half or a rabbit appearing out of thin air, what our eyes see can deceive us. Illusionists and scientists agree: the way perceptions are formed mean we often miss what's in plain view.

Here's why. From the moment we open our eyes, there's a deluge of data. What gets our attention, gets sent to our brains for processing. To make sense of it, we match it to past experiences and beliefs. Next, we interpret it based on factors that include pre-conceived notions, self-concept, values, upbringing, and culture. Essentially, we create a story and stick to it, default to stories that confirm what we already believe to be true and stir in some personal bias.

That means our everyday perception is littered with what psychologists' call "Inattentional blindness," the inability to notice things that are fully visible. If we aren't careful to consider that we have these blind spots, we can miss vital information that reveals opportunities, transforms our awareness and show us the magic glittering before our very eyes.

Insight however is different. It's a deeper intuitive understanding. A new way of viewing the world that reexamines convention and pierces through the darkness —particularly our own. You look past comparison and through a lens of discovery. With practice, insight is a skill that can be learned and once gained, experts say it leads to healthier, stronger, happier lives. I can attest to that.

As a TV Producer for 15 years, my career was based on chasing stories and reporting a range of perspectives, but not until my husband Craig and I created Urban Possibilities, did I experience the real magic of insight. Now we teach it to others. And we found that gem, and so much more, in a place where conventional wisdom would never think to look - Los Angeles' Skid Row.

We started with simple truths, the ones that helped us survive growing up in South Central LA and on the South Side of Chicago respectively like "Success is An Inside Job," "We become what we think" and everyone is born with a unique gift to give this world.

We then built a curriculum and a process that included tests under time constraints and pressure. We road tested it in shelters where people had hit their rock bottom and described themselves as dead. We marveled at what we saw. Real-life inner-city alchemy: Hopelessness converted into effective action; depression turned into determination; Broken heartedness recast into self-actualization; shame into service; Inner darkness turned to light.

I'd always been transfixed by stories of alchemy and just like the fables of old in the quest to follow our hearts we found modern-day magic here in the homeless capital of America. We'd been living in a sea of it all the time. We all are. But our perceptions often forged with misinformation and outdated narratives of who homeless people are, or immigrants, or ex-offenders, or people of color or whatever our blinds spots may be, keep us from seeing the boundless potential in plain sight. Not just in others but in ourselves. Those gaps cause us to miss the opportunity to evolve our thinking, be radically changed by the gifts of our neighbors, be renewed by transcendental hope.

So, as you read the stories and the work of our graduates, we invite you to sit back, open your hearts and see the treasure that's in plain view.

Urban Possibilities in a non-profit empowerment company that equips homeless job seekers and low-income workers with tools to unleash their potential. They have been holding classes in LA's Skid Row community for the past seven years. Through a curriculum that blends success lesson and the arts, each 12-week class culminates with a live performance and book signing of student work. Their mission is to empower people and evolve thinking. www.urbanpossibilities.org

MICHAEL DOUGLAS GRAY

In the trenches of creating Urban Possibilities (UP), we met a soldier who became a warrior for our work. An Air Force veteran gifted with words living at a Los Angeles shelter. Michael Douglas Gray was a student in our first class. A "Men Only" empowerment workshop held on LA's Skid Row to help men who had been through life's worst reconnect to the power within and use it to write a new chapter in their lives.

When we opened the doors to that class, who knew the blessings that would rush in. Michael was chief among them. In him the work took fire. He studied the principles deeply and wrote fearlessly about love, great loss and fatherhood. He was a powerfully eloquent speaker that routinely left us in awe. He was a natural leader who created a strong brotherhood among men, who outside those walls might have been mortal enemies.

Michael inhaled the lessons, put them in practice and was a loving and watchful sentinel for his comrades to do the same. And always he wrote. There were times he couldn't afford to eat but every day he produced pages. About 14 months later after his UP graduation, he self-published his first novel *Pharmekia* and gave us the privilege of seeing what a courageous comeback looks like up close when someone is armed with empowerment tools and their light is turned on. He'd walked through what many could not survive and wrote his way out of it. With pen and in person he stood bravely to tell the story.

He became our champion and worked tirelessly to further this work. He wrote thank you letters to donors, researched grants, spoke at events and constantly brainstormed about how to help us grow. He was spiritual and unselfish, keenly insightful and a man of rare honor.

Michael died suddenly of a massive heart attack while in a class —as always searching for greater truth. He was drafting a plan to launch Urban Possibilities Publishing, his dream to document and distribute the stories of "fallen and forgotten men." He was also just chapters away from completing his second book *The Journey Home*. Although we miss him so much it aches, we also celebrate the life of this student who became our teacher. The man who showed us that our work was far bigger than we imagined—more powerful that we knew.

Michael loved his family and adored his children. So, here's a final gift from our favorite wordsmith. Dedicated to his daughters, he wrote this in that very first class.

AS FATHERS RISE
I can still see her so clearly,
big brown eyes and tiny feet,
the light weight of her on my chest
as we both would fall asleep.

From the start, she was my responsibility.
But I knew that I was lacking
many important qualities.

Memories of her mother's tummy.

Memories of my daughter and me.
Bring joy but now guilt and shame.
Keep joy close company.

You see I've fallen as her father,
but the truth seems to be
that it was necessary
to correct my deficiency.

Be a strong provider,
make her smile and meet her needs.
I must first trust in God our Father
to do the same for me.

Seek him early each morning.
His direction to guide me
with prayer and perseverance,
I will keep growing steadily.

And I will see her again so clearly
older now, same big brown eyes
that once saw her father fallen
and now has seen her father rise.

MARK KERNIZAN

A rising spoken-word artist, Marc Kernizan's stage name is *Sincere Commitment*. "I always wanted a name with purpose. A name that keeps me on the right path." His road to the stage took a circuitous turn, when he landed in Los Angeles and became homeless. "I was meeting teachers, lawyers' people from all walks of life who were homeless, too." For many, shelter living can fracture dreams, but at UP we teach that the thoughts you think are one of the keys to survival. "I would think about how far I've come and what I'm committed to becoming. I would congratulate myself for taking the risk. I've always been a writer, now I'm taking the steps and doing the work to be seen as one." Today, Mark's homeless days are behind him, but serving the homeless is part of his daily life. He works for one of the largest shelters in Los Angeles and is often the first point of contact for those seeking refuge from the streets. "When I was homeless, I thought a lot about who really cares; what kind of person I wanted to be in the future; how I would treat those when I have more, and they have less. I knew I wanted to be of service." He is clear that his art is about giving too. "When I weave words that produce a feeling, it's my way of connecting. It's intimate from my mind and heart to yours. Even if our details are different, there will be things common in our human experience you can relate to. Maybe you won't feel so alone. I didn't choose poetry, it chose me. Now I'm working to use my gift to be a gift to others. For me the seed of it all starts with commitment. Everything grows from there."

Raised in New Jersey by a single mother, Mark was charged at a very young age with the care of his mentally ill older brother. His piece "Hero Here" speaks to that experience.

HERO HERE
HERO here! HERO here!
Innocent, Open and Gleeful,
I'm a child.
HERO here! HERO here!
Remembering my uncontrolled genuine bursts of laughs,
I can feel the, "carefree," in my smile.

HERO here! HERO here!
Daddy's gone, I wonder if I noticed immediately,
I'm still so young.
HERO here! HERO here!
Now, life as a hero has just begun.

HERO here!
I do school, and then do home and school at home.
Helping my older brother learn, what I can,
as much as I can—as I am learning.
The days go by, and the world turns, much like the tides.
My mother has crowned me, "Man of the house."
I wonder what went through my mind.
Maybe a naïve, "she chose me," kind of surprise.
Nothing too disconcerting.

HERO here! HERO here!
I'm taught how to cook – I'm cooking!
House chores, I've learned – I gottem' down.
My brother I babysit at the babysitters,
and there again, when there was no need for babysitters.
He's acting out, I'm looking out.
"Man of the house," I'm so proud.

HERO here! HERO here!
I'm not old, but this, is getting there
Single mother, why does she always call my name?
Why do I always have to do it?
He's not really even trying and lying, "hey that's not fair!"

HERO here!
I'm the "Man of the house," just up until I have a plan,
and then man, "If you wanna be a man you…"
Man, that's a handful and a mouthful,
this is a lot to bear.
But, I'm the man of the house, right?
It's not like, "Poppy's" here.

HERO here! HERO here!
I've had enough, I'm tired.
All of this heavy. I wanna be a little brother,
a Son and the, "Man of the house."
Life, and my mother just won't let me.
"Poppy's" supposed to be here and now it's all on me.
But, "Poppy's," not coming back,
so it falls on me—they call on me!

HERO here!
But they can't see past themselves.
It's taking a toll on me.
I'm getting older now, I hate that they ask for help
and so I ask myself…
Never mind, I keep it pushin'.

Breaking down, but who's looking!?
I hear the talk, get the praise,
but those words can't give me back my days.
I sink in. I'm thinking. I sink in. I sink in.

HERO here!
Depression comes around.
But I'm always here to help.
Now, more and more, I'm in the world – by myself.
I can't tell you who got me – I just know I got myself.
Now I wish a, "Man of the house" was around –
to teach me – how to have my self!

HERO here! HERO here!
Says the little voice,
scream little voice, why won't you speak up.

HERO here! HERO here!
Ready for all who need us.
But always inconsistent, when it's time for us to meet up.

HERO here! HERO here!
What are your fears? I'll help you out. Tell me how you feel?
But if the HERO is always helping the people,
who's helping the HERO heal??

FIND THE WORDS
Write the words that Awaken. Give back what was taken,
Courage. Belief. Understanding. Education.
Write the words that Challenge. To be, or not to be.
Minds need healing. Hearts should be nurtured.
Rhetoric, the pillars that become crutches to assist them further.

Will them through the: Ill will, Ill usions, Ill mannered, Ill lush strious propaganda
To live better today, for better tomorrows—that we may not get to see
To do it for them, because they did it for us. For you. For me.
Write the words that push past egos and pride. That speak confidently against lies.   That look fear in the eye.

Strength. Passion. Determination.
Write the words. Write the words. Write the words that speak a full truth.
The kind that will humble our elders. Prepare our babies. Keep our men secure.
Bring worthiness and esteem, back, to our ladies.

Write the words that lead the youth. Just write the words.
Write the words that bring about a smile.
The kind that make people grimace in pain. That bring them back to life — they live it in vain.

The who, what, when, where
The kind that invoke tears.
Poet. Poetess. Be the student, Life's the test
Put in your everything, bring your best.
Write the words;
Just write the words.

A Harvard graduate with a degree in Economics, Marcia Green also holds a law degree from NYU. When she applied to college, she was accepted at all eight Ivy league schools. Quite a feat for a young woman with undiagnosed learning disabilities that effect both her ability to see and hear. She just worked harder. Always. From day one. "When I was born my umbilical cord wasn't cut correctly so I was bleeding for a really long time. They said a normal child would have stopped crying and died. I just kept crying." Tears became a regular part of Marcia's life. "My father sexually molested me. My family thought I was unattractive and called me horrible names. As a kid I cried a lot. But I had something to prove -that I wasn't just this dark-skinned black girl with nothing to offer. So, I studied and worked twice as hard as the other kids."

That cruelty forged and iron will into steel but as she grew older her body betrayed her. "At Harvard everything fell apart. I had double vision and tracking problems. Vision problems cause organization problems. It became harder to achieve. I couldn't see or hear what my colleagues did, and I felt a lot of humiliation and low-self-esteem." Even with the weight of seeing and hearing disabilities, Marcia's herculean drive earned her a B- average at Harvard and in law school. "As my issues worsened, I couldn't pass the bar and had to look for other work. I eventually became an investigator for the Office of the Federal Public Defender in Los Angeles focusing on death penalty work. Later, I moved to the investigation's unit.

In a car accident, she suffered a traumatic brain injury and was diagnosed in her 50s with lifelong vision disorders and Auditory Processing Disorder. Soon the job she cherished was gone. "I loved my work. I was devasted when it was taken away. I had to sue them for my benefits. Without income, I was terrified that my child and I would become homeless. I didn't have anyone to depend on. Who would hire me? I felt like a complete failure. I had isolated myself. By the time I found Urban Possibilities, I was totally trashed."

"I'd spent much of my career writing about other people's lives in factual reports. I was insecure about expanding my writing but writing creatively feels magical. I give birth to something and it has a life of its own separate from me. I could do something that I thought was really good and I was so proud of that. I think about it a lot. It was always part of me, and I just wrote it down on the page. I also realized I had been a human doing not a human being. That it's all about falling in love with yourself and appreciating your gifts."

After a year of vision and hearing training, Marcia's learning to use her eyes and ears in a new way. She's working again and may soon start teaching. She wants to serve as an inspiration to people with vision and Auditory Processing Disorders to overcome their disabilities and realize their dreams.

I AM ON MY WAY

I am on my way
I am a dreamer who is inspired by the Spirit of my Higher Power in this world
I call on the Higher Power, the ancestors who envelope and support me
Ancestors! Wake up! Rise up! Higher Power!
Ancestors....imbue me with the vision and power to lead me and mine to the Sun.
Ancestors! I feel your power rising up through my feet,
spinning around my calves,
up around my thighs
whirling around my torso,
up through my head
and bursting through to the Sun.

Through the open door
What is on the other side? I see my future but can't seem to let go of the past. My stomach contracts in knots and pressure presses against my skull as I ponder my past. I tearfully and gingerly hold onto my anger and rage.

I open my eyes again. I see it. I smell the clean blue ocean. I breathe in deep. The ocean's briny mist clings to my tongue and lips.

I can return home, but will I? The anger quickly returned when memories of them and what they did to me surface. What they did to everyone. My eyes are closed and burn with rage and impotent fury. I close my eyes and pray for freedom through rescue.

Home is on the other side. I grab the door, and with all my might I throw my stressed-out anxiety ridden body through the door. I land on the sandy beach with a thud.

LARRY BESS, JR.

At 19, Larry Bess, Jr. was sentenced to 16 years in prison. "I made bad choices. I was full of pain and anger for a long time. But now I see the good in what happened. What it taught me about me." Upon release, he stayed with a friend but when violence erupted between two roommates, he googled shelters and made his way to downtown LA.

"Skid Row was a rude awakening. So horrible. Honestly, prison was better. I wouldn't want my worst enemy to experience that. It's a rock bottom place. You could literally go crazy and some people do." He was also coping with being in a world he no longer knew. "When you're released from prison, you're like a fish without water. You have no idea what's going to happen to you. You're in survival mode and depressed. You don't dream or look towards tomorrow. You're just trying to get through the next minute of the day." Larry got into a Skid Row shelter. "I'm grateful I got in, but you are at the mercy of other people and you just do what you are told. On top of that you're fighting a society that doesn't like you because you made a mistake. It's a sad way of life."

A fellow ex-offender invited Larry to an Urban Possibilities class. "He got me there, but the love and support made me stay. I didn't feel like an outsider. It was the one place you could be you. It took me a long time to finish my first piece because I didn't think I had anything to offer. But I saw the class working for others and thought maybe it can work for me too." As Larry dug in, he learned the lessons that would help launch the next chapter of his life. "the class took my excuses away and gave me my voice back. I learned you can't change the past, but I can use it as a motivator. Despite everything, I could stand on my own two feet. We worked as a team and it allowed me to help others and that is the best feeling ever. I knew that is what I'm supposed to be doing"

Today Larry works as a Residential Care Specialist at a recovery facility. "I empower ex-offenders and mental health consumers and teach them to build community in a non-judgmental environment. Every day I use the principles I learned. It's what gets me through. Like circumstances are going to happen, people are going to say things, but you have choice and decision in it all. Now I see that your circumstances are not just about you. It's allowed me to be an example for others. I look back in awe because I help people every day. And the best part is it's not about me. It's so much bigger than that."

FAITH

The subject I know best is faith
that is what drives me to move forward
To accomplish what before seemed like unreachable goals
Even when my negative emotions tell me not to
It is the simple act of faith that fuels me
To forgive others
To forgive myself
And when I feel inadequate and the negative tapes begin to play
It is because of faith
that I am able to not stay stuck in a rut
Or be stuck in yesterday
But rather move forward and evolve into what I was intended to be
And not look back
But forward into tomorrow
For what I have come to believe is
faith is the fuel

That helps me rise above the negative
And motivates me to grow and expand
Into the man I continue to become

SEVEN LETTERS
You can say that you want to quit.
Although you may yell and scream and holler,
And tell yourself there is no use!
Or maybe "woe is me".
My friend, take it from me!
We must never forget
that it is not about how we feel but rather a seven-letter word called "service".
The next time you feel any or all that I have spoken about,
get out of yourself by doing the opposite of what you feel.
By doing the seven letters which we all want to have done to and for us
If you are the one serving, then you will be a blessing
And the problem you thought was a mountain becomes a molehill.
you will be demonstrating the real Jesus in you
while you put these seven letters into sacred action

NORMA "ZAWADI" EATON

As a middle-class woman, Norma "Zawadi" Eaton saw a bright future for herself. She worked solidly as independent contractor in corporate offices that ranged from Toyota to Harbor UCLA Biomedical Institute and made a good salary. She was also a certified make-up artist trained by the Chanel corporation. She and her lover had been together 13 years, living a stone's throw from the beach. But when her partner succumbed to cancer everything changed.

"When my partner died, I was lost. I ended up with an abuser looking for emotional shelter. I went from trauma to trauma. I was in such a fog. Eventually I had to flee for my life leaving everything behind: job, friends, almost everything I owned. I slept in my SUV, called 311 and got into a domestic violence shelter. It was a nightmare. Lock down, lights out, up at 4am to shower and at 5am they would make us clean. They would withhold food; it was like a prison. I had never been exposed to anything like that."

The continual trauma took its toll. "I was numb. I had no feelings. I was totally shut down. My emotions were gone. I couldn't think clearly. I only talked to myself, so I didn't realize my voice was gone too." A requirement of the shelter was that all clients report to a job center. "That's where I was introduced to Urban Possibilities. The first night I attended, no one knew that was the night I was planning to commit suicide. But instead it saved my life. It was the CPR that breathed life back into me class by class."

It took more than six weeks of work for Norma to speak beyond a whisper, but she worked tirelessly to prepare for her graduation performance. "When I took that stage, it was my birthday. And I got so many gifts that healed me that night: People heard me and rejoiced in a standing ovation. The class taught me to persevere and there I was at the finish line. I got my voice back, but it was beyond my current voice, it was the voice that was shut down when I was a child. it, took my shame away and turned what was there into something powerful. I was reborn and became new in this class"

From that day until now, she has dedicated her life to paying it forward as a student mentor, program coordinator and Urban Possibilities spokesperson. She has adopted the name "Zawadi" which means gift which is what she gives audiences when she shares the wisdom gained from surviving some of life's toughest experiences. "Here I learned my story is not bad. I'm not less than. All l I've been through are lessons - it's all fuel. People come in all kinds of prisons and we give them the key to get them out. Facing the truth of who you are takes away the shame. Truth is liberating and I want to share it. I've always loved to serve."

She continues. "Sometimes students are in an ocean drowning but we throw them a life jacket. We can't make them put it on but if they do, we jump in with them. I just want them to see the light and we are that light until they can see it. And light shines in darkness. Even if the light is dim there is hope. We have to show them how to turn that light back on."

Her mission is clear. "At UP I found where I belong and I found my purpose. I'm dedicated to seeing people set free and transformed. I'm here to show students their greatness."

MY NAME IS FORGOTTEN

I would like to leave you with a couple of last words of wisdom. Oh! And just in case you don't know who I am! Or what I look like! My name is forgotten!

Remember me? Let me reintroduce myself. I'm the one you step over twenty-four hours a day, three- hundred and sixty-five days a week

I lay in the middle of your sidewalks, in your train stations, in the streets, parks, dark alleys, bus benches, and sleep in card board boxes.

I'm the one! That points toward the sky, talks to the birds, I curse at the wind, I yell at the walls, question god, why!

I see how you stare with repugnance and disgust as i stroll by your fancy restaurants

I see how you look at me! I realize I'm no longer the beauty queen. Because of the holes in my shoes, the dirt on feet, my matted hair, my overbearing stench is even too much for me to bear.

I had a dream! Just like you! Of one day becoming the president of a fortune 500 company, chief executive officer, doctor or a lawyer, I'm the one that attended Morehouse, Princeton, Stanford, and Harvard. I was the valedictorian, the one voted most likely to succeed! But the cares of this life, and its disappointments took a toll on me

I use to be the one you invited to your Thanksgiving dinners, we held hands, gave thanks and broke bread. I listened to your problems doing whatever I could to solve them

The next time you see me laying in your streets, on bus benches, digging in your trash cans, begging for coins, and you wonder who I am? Take a look in the mirror.

I used to be you!

HAPPY ANNIVERSARY

Six years ago, the essence of my being, was ripped apart
My voice muted to a whisper
Hostage to the negative stories from my trauma
Being deceived by the dark voices of my thoughts.
The pain so great I was making plans to vanish like little vapors dissolving into the universe.
The struggle at times was unbearable
The silence, isolation, sleepless nights
My cup overflowing with tears of sorrow
Landing silently into my pillow
Some days losing my grip on faith
My feet stumbling on hope
Eyes search for refuge, rest,
My broken heart screaming for mercy and grace

But today, all things are new, and I stand in awe! No longer controlled by the traumas of my past. The lessons learned were the compass that guided me through the treacherous storms, over the impossible mountains, and dry valleys

To get me to this place! Where freedom and liberty abide through the empowerment of writing and the magical gift of words. My Oz. Urban Possibilities!

I found the key to unlock my voice, now I speak life, truth, and affirmation. Things that appeared impossible, now knowing that all things being tangible and conceivable

The gift and power of my voice unlocks the door of my future, giving purpose to my dreams, turning my negative story into never-ending possibilities.

I now have a new vision! I have eyes to see beyond the thick fog, to prepare for the abundance available to me.

A new chapter has been written that reads.

A woman chosen to shake up and change the world through her once muted voice. Published writer & poet, storyteller, motivational speaker, associate producer, advocate and activist for those who lost their voice on the road of life.

Who am I? A woman created for greatness! Chosen to live! And I step into that greatness today, this moment, right now!

Happy anniversary world... I'm here!

Urban Possibilities photographs by Craig Johnson